Afternoon tea
at Bramble Cafe

Afternoon tea
at Bramble Cafe

MASTERCHEF UK WINNER 2009
MAT FOLLAS

photography by Steve Painter

RYLAND PETERS & SMALL
LONDON • NEW YORK

Senior designer Toni Kay
Editors Kate Reeves-Brown and
  Miriam Catley
Production controller David Hearn
Art director Leslie Harrington
Editorial director Julia Charles
Publisher Cindy Richards

Photography and prop styling
  Steve Painter
Food stylists Lucy McKelvie and
  Katy Gilhooly
Indexer Vanessa Bird

First published in 2018 by
Ryland Peters & Small
20–21 Jockey's Fields, London WC1R 4BW
and 341 E 116th St, New York NY 10029
www.rylandpeters.com

10 9 8 7 6 5 4 3 2 1

Text copyright © Mat Follas 2018
Design and photographs copyright
© Ryland Peters & Small 2018

ISBN: 978-1-84975-937-3

Printed in China

Notes:
• Both British (Metric) and American
(Imperial plus US cups) measurements
are included in these recipes for your
convenience, however it is important
to work with one set of measurements
only and not alternate between the
two within a recipe.
• All spoon measurements are level
unless otherwise specified. A teaspoon
is 5 ml, a tablespoon is 15 ml.
• All eggs are medium (UK) or large (US),
unless specified as large, in which case
US extra-large should be used. Uncooked
or partially cooked eggs should not be
served to the very old, frail, young
children, pregnant women or those
with compromised immune systems.
• Ovens should be preheated to the
specified temperatures. We recommend
using an oven thermometer. If using a
fan-assisted oven, adjust temperatures
according to the manufacturer's
instructions.

Contents

Introduction

I grew up in New Zealand, with all of its wonderful Pan-Asian influences, and yet, the food I love and come back to time and time again, is traditional, English fare.

I guess it's the influence of key personalities in my childhood that runs the deepest. I remember going for afternoon tea with my grandmother in the cafe in Cornwall Park, Auckland. As a child, it felt like entering another world; one where the pace was slower, the tea was served in teapots, and the cakes looked like little works of art. Afternoon tea is a childhood memory I treasure. These days, I'm lucky enough to live in the heart of the English countryside and have a traditional English cafe in the county town where Thomas Hardy lived; Gran would have loved it.

There is, normally, a fantastic sense of satisfaction that comes from baking something delicious; whether it's a simple biscuit, or something a bit more complicated. Nothing beats the aroma as your baking comes out of the oven, or the smiles you get when it's eaten.

The recipes in this book include some of the most well-known cafe classics. When I was thinking about opening Bramble Cafe, these 'firm favourites' were the recipes I wrote first and they've gradually evolved over the last few years into easy, foolproof, well-tested recipes.

Many of the cake recipes are as simple as measuring the ingredients and mixing until combined. In most cases there's no creaming, or adding one egg at a time, I don't have the patience for all that, or the attention span, so everything is designed to be as quick and easy as possible.

Bramble Cafe opened in 2016 and was a massive departure from the fine dining restaurant I had run previously. I wanted to cook comfort food and provide an atmosphere of calm familiarity to enjoy it in. I wanted a very customer-friendly alternative to the counter service queuing of modern coffee shops. A small lunchtime menu of traditional delights that you'll come back for time after time. In the afternoons, we love to serve an afternoon tea, with selections of cakes, scones, treats, savouries, a light cocktail or tea and coffee; it doesn't matter what your choices are but it does matter that it's all delicious and fun to eat.

At the cafe we serve simple food, made with great quality ingredients. Much of our food is handmade in-house using ingredients from local producers and we make most of our own jams, chutneys, pickles and sauces.

Just like in the pages of this book, there are little influences of my New Zealand upbringing throughout the menu but the predominant theme is delightful, simple, English dishes.

Some of the recipes included here are my versions of classics, Anzac Biscuits and a Victoria Sandwich, for example, but I've tried to give you tweaks that make the ingredients easier to measure and the baking more reliable. I've updated recipes to metric measurements to help when using digital kitchen scales.

I can't stress enough the need for fresh ingredients. Eggs that are super fresh will make your cakes rise and hold incredibly well. If you're using eggs from a supermarket, use an extra pinch of baking powder in the cake recipes.

Baking is a form of chemistry, so scales and accurate temperatures are very important for perfect bakes. Simple digital scales will give you reliable results every time and a probe thermometer will tell you when things are properly baked, whereas using a skewer only checks a small part of the cake. My advice would also be to spend a few pounds/dollars and get an oven thermometer.

I've used self-raising/self-rising flour for many recipes. If you don't have any, you can use regular flour and sift in a level teaspoon of baking powder for every 150 g/1 cup plain/all-purpose flour, as an alternative. If you do this, remember to only use plain/all-purpose flour, as flours for bread-making will make your cakes tough and not rise as well. To tell the difference, look at the percentage of protein in the flour; for baking it should be below 10%.

We make many of our cakes for Bramble Cafe using gluten-free ingredients. So, while this book has not set out to be a gluten-free recipe book, most of the slices, biscuits and denser cakes, like my carrot cake, can be made using the better gluten-free flour mixes and are almost indistinguishable from those made using regular flour. I add one level teaspoon of xanthan gum powder to every 250 g/1¾ cups gluten-free self-raising/self-rising flour and I often add a few dessertspoons of natural/plain yogurt to the cakes and slices to add extra flavour.

I hope you enjoy this book and nothing would give me more pleasure than to be sent a picture of your dog-eared, flour splattered, used regularly, copy. Cookbooks are meant to be used, not kept pristine, so please put this beside your blender, choose a recipe and start cooking!

How to make the perfect cup of afternoon tea

How to make the perfect cup of tea, for all varieties of tea, is not something I can realistically cover in a few words here. Whole books are dedicated to tea making. What I can talk about is my view of how to make the perfect cup of afternoon tea.

A pot of afternoon tea should always be a blend of Assam Indian tea leaves; one teaspoon per person and one for the teapot is a good rule of thumb. You might like it a little stronger, if so, add another teaspoon.

The tea is made with just-boiled water and left for about 3 minutes before serving. Tradition demands that, for luck, the teapot is turned around three times in a clockwise direction during this time, I remember my Grandmother always doing this.

Assam tea is served with a dash of milk in the teacup before the tea is poured. Sugar is optional but really should be used only in the morning, as afternoon tea should always be served with sweet treats.

A pot of Earl Grey tea is also ideal for drinking with afternoon tea; the bergamot zest in the tea leaves gives the tea a lovely zesty and floral flavour. It should be served with similar amounts of tea per teapot to the Assam tea, but with a tiny slice of lemon in the teacup, not milk.

All of the above said, do make your tea how you like it. Add milk to your Earl Grey, pour the milk after the tea or add sugar... it's your cup of tea after all.

How to make the perfect cup of coffee

To make the perfect coffee is similarly complex in its techniques and varieties as tea. Each culture has a different method of making coffee from traditional thick, gritty, sweet Turkish coffee to the modern cold extraction methods of trendy coffee shops, all delicious but so very different. Assuming you have access to a decent espresso maker, here is my suggested method of making coffee.

The coffee shot should be made from about 20 g/ ¼ cup finely ground coffee beans to produce about 40–45 g/1½ oz. of espresso coffee. It should take about 25 seconds to make. It's worth spending some time to 'tune' your coffee maker. Adjust your grind until you are achieving this time and weight and you will have a smooth, full-flavoured, double espresso shot of coffee. It goes without saying that you should only use a good-quality roasted coffee; I prefer a medium roast.

The espresso shot can be drunk on its own, but I would drink it like this only in the morning. For afternoon tea, I would pour over 50 ml/3½ tablespoons of just-boiled water to make a 'long black', or make a latte or flat white coffee.

To make a latte or flat white, hot milk is added to the cup after the espresso. A latte uses about 250 ml/1 cup steamed milk and a flat white uses about 150 ml/⅔ cup. The milk is steamed using a steam wand in a metal jug/pitcher. Cup the jug/pitcher in your hand and steam the milk in a swirling motion until it is just too hot to touch; about 55°C/130°F. This temperature will create micro bubbles in the milk giving it a smooth, almost silky, texture. Pour the steamed milk over the espresso shot. With practice, you'll be able to make patterns with the milk like your local coffee shop does.

As with the tea, feel free to ignore most of what I have written and make coffee in your preferred way, but please do try it my way and adapt from there to suit your taste.

Hot chocolate

When we first opened Bramble Cafe, we used to buy very expensive hot chocolate mixes, but have since discovered that we can easily make it ourselves using a good-quality chocolate. With a good chocolate, it won't need any sugar. I prefer using dark/bittersweet chocolate in my hot chocolate, but the majority of our customers prefer milk chocolate. The chocolate powder keeps well in a cool place, stored in an airtight container.

PREPARE 5 MINUTES / COOK 5 MINUTES

CHOCOLATE POWDER
200 g/7 oz. chilled milk or dark/ bittersweet chocolate

VARIATIONS
1 teaspoon ground cinnamon
2 teaspoons hot chilli/chili powder
50 g/2 oz. extra strong peppermints
grated zest of 2 oranges

TO SERVE (PER CUP)
200 ml/generous ¾ cup milk
30 ml/2 tablespoons double/ heavy cream
unsweetened cocoa powder (optional)
mini marshmallows (optional)
whipped cream (optional)

To make the chocolate powder, use a food processor with a grating/shredding attachment. Put the chocolate through the grater in small pieces, so it doesn't melt or stick together from the friction. It should become the consistency of finely grated/ shredded hard cheese.

If you want to try a variation, then use one of the suggestions and combine with the ground chocolate. For the mint hot chocolate, run the peppermints through the grating/ shredding attachment, too, to turn them into powder.

Keep the chocolate mix cool and sealed until ready to use.

To make a hot chocolate
If you have access to a steam wand on a coffee machine, pour the milk and 4 teaspoons of the chocolate mixture into a mug. Steam to dissolve the chocolate. Add the cream and stir to finish.

If you don't have access to a steam wand, pour the cream and 4 teaspoons of the chocolate mixture into a mug. Heat for about 20 seconds in a microwave until the chocolate dissolves. Stir to combine, before adding the milk and again heating in a microwave until it reaches drinking temperature.

Serve as it is, sprinkle with a little cocoa powder, or dress it up with marshmallows and whipped cream for a real treat!

Cakes & scones

Lemon drizzle cake

I made no less than 12 different lemon drizzle cakes when we were thinking about opening the cafe. It's my first choice of cake with a morning cuppa, so I wanted to get it just right. This recipe is bulletproof and requires very little work as long as you weigh accurately and use fresh eggs. This recipe is also dairy free for any lactose intolerant guests.

PREPARE 10 MINUTES / COOK 60–70 MINUTES

CAKE
5 eggs
approx. 250 g/scant 2 cups
self-raising/self-rising flour
approx. 250 ml/1 cup plus
1 tablespoon vegetable oil
approx. 250 g/1¼ cups caster/
granulated sugar
grated zest of 2 lemons

DRIZZLE
freshly squeezed juice of 2 lemons
50 g/¼ cup caster/granulated sugar,
plus extra for sprinkling

non-stick 900-g/2-lb. loaf pan, lightly
oiled and lined with baking parchment

SERVES 8

Preheat the oven to 140°C (280°F) Gas 1.

Place your mixing bowl onto your scales and zero the scales. Into the bowl, crack the eggs and make a note of the weight. Add the same weight of flour, oil and sugar, then add the lemon zest.

Mix for a few minutes with a hand-held electric whisk or in a stand mixer until it forms a smooth batter. Pour into the lined loaf pan, then place in the preheated oven for 60 minutes, until a skewer poked into the centre comes out clean and the internal temperature reaches 90°C/195°F.

Leave the cake to cool for 20 minutes.

For the drizzle, heat the lemon juice and sugar in a saucepan until the sugar is dissolved.

To finish, use a skewer to make holes in the top of the cake. Drizzle the lemon syrup into the holes and over the top of the cake to infuse the cake with lemon. Remove the cake from the loaf pan and sprinkle a little caster/granulated sugar over the top of the cake to form a lemon crust.

Katy's apple cake

In a county where most apples are used in cider production, it is almost a requirement for any baker to save a few for making a Dorset apple cake. Dorset families can be split over whether to add sultanas/golden raisins to the cake, or not (we don't). Ours also breaks traditional rules with the addition of a little spice, but the results are worth it. Katy opened Bramble Cafe with my wife and me, and this is her prized recipe.

PREPARE 10 MINUTES / COOK 60 MINUTES

CAKE
6 eggs
approx. 300 g/2¼ cups self-raising/ self-rising flour
approx. 300 ml/1¼ cups vegetable oil
approx. 300 g/1½ cups golden caster/granulated sugar
2 teaspoons five-spice powder
2 Granny Smith apples

TOPPING
100 ml/generous ⅓ cup apple juice
50 g/¼ cup brown muscovado sugar

non-stick 25-cm/10-inch round cake pan, lightly greased with butter and base-lined with baking parchment

SERVES 10

Preheat the oven to 140°C (280°F) Gas 1.

Place a mixing bowl onto your scales and set them to zero. Into the bowl, crack the eggs and make a note of the weight. Add the same weight of flour, oil and sugar, then add the five-spice powder. Mix for a few minutes with a hand-held electric whisk or in a stand mixer until it forms a smooth batter.

Peel, core and dice the apples into approx. 5-mm/¼-inch cubes, add to the batter and mix together. Pour into the lined cake pan and place in the preheated oven for 50 minutes.

To make the topping, in a saucepan, heat the apple juice and 25 g/2 tablespoons of the muscovado sugar until it has melted and forms a syrup.

After 50 minutes, check the cake has risen and has a firm top. The internal temperature should be just over 80°C/175°F. Brush the top with the topping syrup, then place the cake back in the oven for another 10 minutes to finish baking. The cake is cooked when a skewer poked into the centre comes out clean and the internal temperature reaches 90°C/195°F.

Leave the cake to cool for 20 minutes, then remove from the cake pan, dust with the remaining muscovado sugar and leave to cool on a wire rack.

Best served warm with whipped cream.

pictured page 20

Chocolate & vanilla marble cake

Always a fun cake for the display in the cafe or for afternoon tea, a marble cake is not to be taken too seriously. The challenge as a cook is to keep the cake moist and to make each flavour distinctive. Experiment with different combinations to make fun colour mixes, raspberry and lime is a favourite of mine and looks amazing. I add a little extra milk to my chocolate sponge mix as cocoa will dry out a cake without some extra moisture to compensate.

PREPARE 20 MINUTES / COOK 70–90 MINUTES

BASIC SPONGE
5 eggs
approx. 250 g/scant 2 cups
 self-raising/self-rising flour
approx. 250 ml/1 cup plus
 1 tablespoon vegetable oil
approx. 250 g/1¼ cups caster/
 granulated sugar

VANILLA SPONGE
1 teaspoon pure vanilla extract

CHOCOLATE SPONGE
4 teaspoons unsweetened
 cocoa powder
50 ml/3½ tablespoons milk

non-stick 900-g/2-lb. loaf pan, lightly
 oiled and lined with baking parchment

SERVES 12

Preheat the oven to 140°C (280°F) Gas 1.

Place your mixing bowl onto your scales and zero the scales. Into the bowl, crack the eggs and make a note of the weight. Add the same weight of each of the flour, oil and sugar.

Mix for a few minutes with a hand-held electric whisk or in a stand mixer until it forms a smooth batter.

Divide the cake mixture equally between two mixing bowls. Fold the vanilla extract into one portion and fold the cocoa powder and milk into the other portion.

Now, alternating large spoonfuls of each mixture, dollop the sponge mixes into the lined loaf pan until all the mixture has been used. Place in the preheated oven for 70–90 minutes, until a skewer poked into the centre comes out clean and the internal temperature reaches 90°C/195°F.

Leave the cake to cool for 20 minutes before removing from the pan.

Serve in thin slices.

pictured page 21

Victoria sandwich

Victoria sandwich is the classic afternoon cake, and is made using the freshest of cream and strawberry jam/jelly. I use the 'all-in' method of mixing my flour, butter, sugar and eggs, rather than the traditional method of beating the butter and sugar together first; it's not necessary if your eggs are super fresh.

PREPARE 20 MINUTES / COOK 25–30 MINUTES

CAKE

5 eggs

approx. 250 g/scant 2 cups self-raising/self-rising flour

approx. 250 g/2¼ sticks butter, softened

approx. 250 g/1¼ cups caster/ granulated sugar

1 teaspoon pure vanilla extract

STRAWBERRIES AND CREAM FILLING

200 g/2 cups fresh strawberries

freshly squeezed juice of 1 lemon

50 g/¼ cup caster/granulated sugar

300 ml/1¼ cups whipping cream

50 g/6 tablespoons icing/ confectioners' sugar, plus extra for dusting

1 teaspoon pure vanilla extract

2 x 25-cm/10-inch round cake pans, lightly oiled and lined with baking parchment (single layer on the base and a double/ folded layer around the sides)

SERVES 10

Preheat the oven to 140°C (280°F) Gas 1.

Place the mixing bowl onto the scales and zero the scales. Into the bowl, crack the eggs and make a note of the weight. Add the same weight of flour, softened butter and caster/granulated sugar.

Mix for a few minutes with a hand-held electric whisk or in a stand mixer until it just forms a smooth batter.

Add the vanilla extract and mix for another minute to combine. Divide the mixture between the two lined cake pans, then place in the preheated oven for 25–30 minutes. Do not open your oven for any reason for at least 20 minutes, or the cakes may collapse!

The cakes are cooked when a skewer poked into the centre comes out clean and the internal temperature reaches 90°C/195°F. Remove from the oven immediately when this temperature is reached, so the cakes don't dry out.

Leave the cakes to cool for 20 minutes before removing from the pans as this will complete the baking but keep the cakes moist. Transfer to a wire rack to cool completely.

For the filling, chop the strawberries into small pieces and place in a mixing bowl with the lemon juice and caster/granulated sugar. Mix together and leave for at least 20 minutes before using on the cake.

Whip the cream, icing/confectioners' sugar and vanilla extract together until it forms, and holds, soft peaks.

Level the top, if necessary, of one of the cakes using a bread knife. Place the strawberries on the levelled top. Turn the other half over and spread the cream generously on the flat side. Place the top, cream-side down, onto the strawberry-coated half. Dust with icing/confectioners' sugar.

Ultimate chocolate fudge cake

We use this recipe as our go-to birthday cake. Melted fudge and dark/bittersweet chocolate combine to make this rich and indulgent.

PREPARE 30 MINUTES / COOK 35–40 MINUTES

CAKE

200 g/7 oz. vanilla fudge
200 ml/generous ¾ cup milk
4 eggs
approx. 200 ml/scant 1 cup
    vegetable oil
approx. 200 g/1 cup caster/
    granulated sugar
approx. 300 g/2¼ cups self-raising/
    self-rising flour
100 ml/⅓ cup natural/plain yogurt
50 g/½ cup unsweetened cocoa
    powder
1 teaspoon baking powder

FROSTING

150 g/5¼ oz. dark/bittersweet
    chocolate
250 g/2¼ sticks butter, softened
300 g/2 cups icing/confectioners'
    sugar, sifted
25 g/¼ cup unsweetened cocoa
    powder
1 teaspoon pure vanilla extract

TOPPINGS

spray glitter, mini chocolate
    cigarellos, fudge pieces or
    kirsch cherries

*2 x 25-cm/10-inch round cake pans, lightly
oiled and lined with baking parchment
(single layer on the base and a double/
folded layer around the sides)*

SERVES 10

Preheat the oven to 140°C (280°F) Gas 1.

For the cake, in a small saucepan, melt the fudge and milk over a low heat and whisk together to combine fully.

Place a mixing bowl onto the scales and zero the scales. Into the bowl, crack the eggs and make a note of the weight. Add the same weight of oil and caster/granulated sugar. Add the same weight of flour, plus another 100 g/¾ cup of flour. Add the yogurt, then sift and add the cocoa and baking powders. Mix for a few minutes with a hand-held electric whisk or in a stand mixer until it just forms a smooth batter.

Check the fudge and milk mixture has cooled enough to be able to touch it, then add it to the mixing bowl and fold together to combine.

Divide the mixture between the two lined cake pans, then place in the preheated oven for 35–40 minutes, until a skewer poked into the centre comes out clean and the internal temperature reaches 90°C/195°F. Remove from the oven immediately. Leave the cakes to cool for 20 minutes before removing from the pans. Transfer to a wire rack to cool completely.

For the frosting, place the chocolate in a microwaveable bowl and melt. Start with a 30-second burst in the microwave on high, then stir. Keep heating in 10-second bursts and stirring until it is nearly all melted. Use a rubber spatula to beat the chocolate to form a smooth, glossy chocolate.

In a stand mixer, beat the butter and sifted icing/confectioners' sugar together, until fully combined. Sift in the cocoa and beat before adding the melted chocolate and vanilla. Beat again to fully combine the ingredients.

To finish, use a bread knife to slice the domed top off one of the cakes. Spread about one-quarter of the frosting over the top. Place the other cake on top. Spread a very thin layer of frosting over the whole cake, pressing it into the cake surface. Remove any excess frosting and place in the refrigerator for 20 minutes to set. Smooth over the remainder of the frosting, then let your imagination take over and add any of the toppings you like – glitter, mini chocolate cigarellos, fudge pieces or kirsch cherries.

Rainbow cake

Colourful and fun, this is a cake with which you can let your imagination run wild. Try different flavour and colour combinations of cake and frosting. Use specialist cake colours as regular ones just don't seem to work when baked.

PREPARE 40 MINUTES / COOK 12–15 MINUTES

4 eggs
approx. 200 g/1½ cups self-raising/
    self-rising flour
approx. 200 ml/scant 1 cup
    vegetable oil
200 g/1 cup caster/granulated sugar
yellow, red and blue cake colourings
½ teaspoon pure vanilla extract
concentrated lemon flavour
concentrated raspberry flavour
concentrated liquorice flavour

BUTTERCREAM
100 g/7 tablespoons butter,
    softened
250 g/1¾ cups icing/confectioners'
    sugar, plus extra for dusting
1 teaspoon pure vanilla extract
2–3 tablespoons warm water

4 non-stick 20-cm/8-inch round cake
    pans, lightly oiled and lined with
    baking parchment

SERVES 10

Preheat the oven to 140°C (280°F) Gas 1.

For the cake, place your mixing bowl onto the scales and zero the scales. Into the bowl, crack the eggs and make a note of the weight. Add the same weight of flour, oil and caster/granulated sugar.

Mix for a few minutes with a hand-held electric whisk or in a stand mixer until it just forms a smooth batter.

Take three more mixing bowls and, using the scales, divide the cake mixture evenly between the four bowls. You will now have four mixing bowls containing equal amounts of cake mixture.

To the first bowl add ½ teaspoon pure vanilla extract. To the second bowl add yellow cake colouring and a few drops of the lemon flavour. To the third bowl add red cake colouring and a few drops of the raspberry flavour. To the fourth bowl add blue cake colouring and a few drops of the liquorice flavour. Fold the colour and flavouring into the mixtures until fully combined, then pour each into a prepared cake pan.

Place the filled cake pans in the preheated oven and bake for 12–15 minutes. Do not open your oven for any reason for at least 10 minutes or they may collapse! The cakes are cooked when a skewer inserted into the centre comes out cleanly and the internal temperature reaches 90°C/195°F. Remove from the oven immediately once this temperature is reached, so the cakes don't dry out. Leave the cakes to cool in the pans for 10 minutes, then place on a wire rack to cool completely.

For the buttercream, in a mixing bowl, whisk the softened butter, icing/confectioners' sugar and vanilla together until the mixture is smooth, then add the warm water while whisking to lighten the buttercream.

Using a bread knife, level the blue, red and yellow cake layers. Generously ice each of the three layers and stack them on top of one another. To finish the cake, place the white cake layer on top and dust with icing/confectioners' sugar.

Sticky gingerbread

Sticky, sweet, spicy ginger cake, served slathered in butter and still warm from the oven, on an autumnal/fall afternoon with a pot of Assam tea, is about as good as afternoon tea gets.

PREPARE 20 MINUTES / COOK 60–70 MINUTES

100 g/7 tablespoons butter

100 g/5 tablespoons golden/
light corn syrup

100 g/5 tablespoons black treacle/
molasses

100 g/½ cup soft dark brown sugar

200 g/1½ cups self-raising/self-
rising flour

2 tablespoons five-spice powder

2 teaspoons ground ginger

100 g/3½ oz. stem ginger,
finely chopped

1 egg

250 ml/1 cup milk

non-stick 900-g/2-lb. loaf pan, lightly oiled and lined with baking parchment

SERVES 8

Preheat the oven to 140°C (280°F) Gas 1.

In a heavy-bottomed saucepan, melt the butter, golden/light corn syrup, black treacle/molasses and brown sugar on a low heat, stirring to combine.

In a mixing bowl, combine the flour, five-spice powder and ground ginger and stir to combine. Add the stem ginger and mix, ensuring the ginger pieces are coated with the flour mixture and not clumped together.

Whisk the egg and milk together.

Add the melted ingredients to the flour mixture in the mixing bowl and fold together to combine. Add the whisked milk and egg mixture whilst continuing to fold together, until you have a smooth, even batter.

Pour the batter into the lined loaf pan and place in the preheated oven for 60–70 minutes, until a skewer poked into the centre comes out clean and the internal temperature reaches 90°C/195°F.

Remove from the oven and leave the cake to cool for 20 minutes before removing from the pan.

Serve in generous slices with plenty of butter.

Banana loaf

This cake would be a great option for people who are on a diet because of its much-reduced sugar and oil content... although I would advise trying a slice with a generous amount of butter, so maybe not. Whether you're cutting back the calories or not, you won't be disappointed with the flavour and moistness of this loaf.

PREPARE 10 MINUTES / COOK 50–60 MINUTES

250 g/generous 1¾ cups self-
  raising/self-rising flour
100 g/½ cup caster/granulated
  sugar
75 g/⅓ cup vegetable oil
50 ml/3½ tablespoons milk
200 g/7 oz. banana, mashed
  (2 large bananas)
2 eggs
1 teaspoon ground cinnamon
butter, to serve

*non-stick 900-g/2-lb. loaf pan, lightly
  oiled and lined with baking parchment*

SERVES 8

Preheat the oven to 140°C (280°F) Gas 1.

Place all the ingredients into a large mixing bowl. Mix for a few minutes with a hand-held electric whisk or in a stand mixer, until it forms a smooth batter.

Pour the mixture into the lined loaf pan, then place in the preheated oven for 50–60 minutes, until a skewer poked into the centre comes out clean and the internal temperature reaches 90°C/195°F.

Remove the loaf from the oven and leave to cool for at least 20 minutes before removing and slicing.

Serve buttered.

Fruit cake

A good fruit cake takes time, and alcohol. Soaking the fruit overnight in brandy gives this cake a naughty but delicious flavour. Leave in the refrigerator for a week before icing, 'feeding' it every couple of days with about 4 teaspoons of brandy.

PREPARE 30 MINUTES / COOK 150 MINUTES

200 g/scant 1½ cups sultanas/ golden raisins

200 g/scant 1½ cups (dark) raisins

50 g/generous ⅓ cup dried mixed peel

200 g/1½ cups stoned/pitted dates, chopped

200 ml/generous ¾ cup brandy

250 g/1¼ cups Demerara sugar

250 g/2¼ sticks butter, softened

4 eggs

200 g/1½ cups self-raising/ self-rising flour

50 g/½ cup ground almonds

grated zest of 1 lemon

1 teaspoon pure vanilla extract

30-cm/12-inch round cake pan, buttered and lined with baking parchment (to stop the edges drying out, add two further layers of paper on the outside of the pan, which rise above the top of the tin by at least 2.5 cm/1 inch; tie the outer layers of paper with cooking twine to hold in place)

SERVES 10

Preheat the oven to 120°C (250°F) Gas 1.

The night before, place the sultanas/golden raisins, (dark) raisins, mixed peel and chopped dates in a container and cover them with the brandy.

The next day, place the sugar and butter in a large bowl. Whisk with a hand-held electric whisk until the mixture is creamy and has increased in volume by about half. Add the eggs, one at a time, and 2 teaspoons of the flour, and continue whisking until a smooth mixture is formed.

Add the remaining flour and ground almonds, and fold together. Add the lemon zest and the vanilla extract whilst continuing to fold together. Finally, drain the soaked fruit (reserving the brandy and setting it aside for later), and add the fruit to the mixture. Fold together to combine thoroughly.

Pour the mixture into the prepared cake pan and bake in the preheated oven for 2½ hours, until a skewer poked into the centre comes out clean and the internal temperature reaches 95°C/205°F.

Remove carefully from the oven and leave to cool for at least 30 minutes before removing from the cake pan. Transfer to a wire rack and cool completely.

Wrap the cold cake in baking parchment and foil. Poke small holes in the top of the cake and pour over the reserved brandy before sealing with foil.

Leave in the refrigerator overnight before serving.

Plain scones

Plain scones are anything but! They are light, buttery, melt in the mouth, a mini meal, perfectly complemented by some homemade jam. You know you have achieved perfect scones when they form a natural crack in the middle when they're baked, so you can just pull them in two. Be careful not to overwork the dough or they will not rise.

PREPARE 10 MINUTES / COOK 12–14 MINUTES

500 g/3¾ cups self-raising/
   self-rising flour, plus extra for
   dusting
100 g/7 tablespoons butter, chilled
30 g/2½ tablespoons caster/
   granulated sugar
100 ml/⅓ cup milk
100 ml/⅓ cup double/heavy cream
100 g/¾ cup sultanas/golden
   raisins (optional)
1 egg yolk

7.5-cm/3-inch cookie cutter

MAKES 8 SCONES

Preheat the oven to 220°C (425°F) Gas 7.

Add the flour, small pieces of butter (each approx. 20 g/ 1½ tablespoons) and the sugar to a food processor and pulse until they form a crumb.

Continue pulsing the mixture whilst adding the milk and then the cream in a steady stream, until the mixture forms a dough ball that just holds together.

Lightly flour your hands and a cool, flat surface (marble is ideal). Fold the sultanas/golden raisins into the dough, if using. Press the dough out to about a thickness of 5 cm/2 inches. Use the cookie cutter to cut out the scones. Re-press the leftover dough together to maximize the number of scones, but always use the cutter to form sharp edges or the scones will not rise properly.

Make a glaze by whisking the egg yolk and brush the tops only with the glaze.

Bake for 12–14 minutes until just cooked through and risen. I always carefully split one scone to check the centre is cooked.

Strawberries & cream Swiss roll

There are only three ingredients in a classic Swiss/jelly roll (plus the filling): flour, sugar and eggs. A Swiss roll can be a dry cake as no oils have been used in the baking, so compensate with fresh fruit and indulge in a little extra cream.

PREPARE 20 MINUTES / COOK 12–14 MINUTES

FILLING
200 g/2 cups strawberries
freshly squeezed juice of ½ lemon
30 g/2½ tablespoons caster/
    granulated sugar
150 ml/²/₃ cup whipping cream
½ teaspoon pure vanilla extract
50 g/6 tablespoons icing/
    confectioners' sugar

CAKE
200 g/7 oz. eggs, lightly whisked
    with 150 g/³/₄ cup caster/
    granulated sugar
1 teaspoon pure vanilla extract
150 g/generous 1 cup plain/
    all-purpose or sponge flour

icing/confectioners' sugar and
    fresh strawberries, to decorate

45 x 30-cm/18 x 12-inch non-stick Swiss roll/jelly roll pan, lightly oiled and base-lined with baking parchment

MAKES 1 ROLL

Preheat the oven to 140°C (280°F) Gas 1.

For the filling, hull and finely chop the strawberries. Place them in a bowl and fold in the lemon juice and caster/granulated sugar. Leave for 30 minutes to bring out the flavour. Whip the cream, vanilla extract and icing/confectioners' sugar to a light, just setting, whipped cream. Chill.

For the cake, take the prepared Swiss roll/jelly roll pan, oil the top of the paper and lightly flour the paper and the sides. Place the whisked eggs and caster/granulated sugar in a bowl and mix for at least 10 minutes with a hand-held electric whisk or in a stand mixer, until it has tripled in volume and is thick and creamy. Add the vanilla extract and whisk.

Gently fold in the flour, one-third at a time, until just combined.

Pour the mixture into the prepared Swiss roll/jelly roll pan and use a spatula to spread it to an even depth. Immediately place the pan into the oven and bake for 12 minutes. Check the cake is cooked by touch; it should bounce back when lightly pressed. If it is soft or it 'crackles' when touched, put it back in the oven for 2 minutes more, then check again.

Remove from the oven and leave to cool for 2 minutes. Cover a wire rack with a piece of oiled and floured baking parchment and, carefully, turn the cake out onto the rack. Leave the cake to cool for 5 minutes.

While the cake is still a little warm, carefully peel the baking parchment off. Gently cut halfway through the cake, across the width of the cake, on the short side, about 1 cm/½ inch from the edge, this will help it roll up.

Starting from the side where you have made the cut, carefully roll up the cake and gently squeeze it to form the roll, before unrolling again in order to assemble the final cake.

Finish the filling by folding together the whipped cream and strawberries. Plaster the mixture generously onto the cake, then carefully roll up to make a Swiss/jelly roll. Trim the ends off to make a neat finish and dust with icing/confectioners' sugar.

Slices & tarts

Brownies

There's an art to making the perfect gooey, crunchy brownie. The gooeyness is all about timing, using a thermometer takes the guesswork out of this. The key to the crunchy top is whisking your eggs until they are foaming and hold their bubbles and, most importantly, using the freshest eggs you can find. These brownies also work well using a good-quality gluten-free flour.

PREPARE 15 MINUTES / COOK 20–25 MINUTES

BROWNIE
300 g/2¾ sticks butter
300 g/10½ oz. good-quality
  dark/bittersweet chocolate
5 eggs
400 g/2 cups caster/granulated
  sugar
30 g/⅓ cup unsweetened cocoa
  powder
150 g/1 generous cup plain/
  all-purpose flour or
  gluten-free flour

RASPBERRY BROWNIES
200 g/1⅓ cups raspberries
50 g/¼ cup caster/granulated sugar
freshly squeezed juice of ½ lemon

*non-stick 30 x 20-cm/12 x 8-inch
  brownie pan, lightly oiled and
  lined with baking parchment*

MAKES 10 BROWNIES

Preheat the oven to 140°C (280°F) Gas 1.

For the brownie, place the butter in a saucepan and melt over a low heat. Once the butter is fully melted, break the chocolate up into individual pieces and add to the melted butter. Leave for a few minutes, then stir together to form a thick chocolate ganache sauce. Leave the sauce to cool for 20 minutes.

Place the eggs and sugar in a large mixing bowl and whisk using a hand-held electric whisk until thick, smooth and creamy. Add the chocolate sauce and the cocoa, and whisk to combine the ingredients until the mixture is thick and even. With a wooden spoon, fold in the flour until the mixture is smooth.

Pour the brownie mixture into the lined brownie pan and bake in the preheated oven for 20–25 minutes. The brownies are cooked when the mixture has a core temperature of 90°C/195°F; they should still have a little bit of a wobble. Cool for 30 minutes at room temperature. To slice without cracking the top too much, chill in the refrigerator for a few hours before cutting.

To serve, reheat for 15 seconds in a microwave and serve with cream or ice cream.

Raspberry brownies

Place the raspberries in a bowl with the sugar and lemon juice in advance. Stir, then leave to infuse for 30 minutes or longer. Place the raspberries in the brownie pan before you add the brownie mixture. Carefully cover them with the brownie mixture (if they poke through the top they will catch and burn).

Millionaire's shortbread

I can get my teenage son to do any chore for the reward of a piece of millionaire's shortbread. It takes a little time to make, but each stage is quick and fairly simple. The topping can be milk chocolate instead of dark/bittersweet, if you prefer, and with a drizzle of white chocolate, it looks amazing.

PREPARE 30 MINUTES / COOK 45 MINUTES

SHORTBREAD
175 g/1⅓ cups plain/all-purpose flour
75 g/¾ cup cornflour/cornstarch
150 g/1¼ sticks butter, chilled and diced into small pieces
75 g/6 tablespoons caster/granulated sugar

CARAMEL
100 g/7 tablespoons butter
100 g/½ cup golden caster/granulated sugar
400-g/14-oz can condensed milk

CHOCOLATE
300 g/10½ oz. dark/bittersweet chocolate
50 ml/3½ tablespoons double/heavy cream

non-stick 30 x 20-cm/12 x 8-inch brownie pan, lightly oiled and lined with baking parchment

MAKES ABOUT 24

Preheat the oven to 160°C (325°F) Gas 3.

For the shortbread, in a food processor, blitz all the shortbread ingredients briefly to make a crumb. Pour the crumb mix over the base of the prepared brownie pan and press it down lightly.

Place in the preheated oven and bake for 20 minutes, until the shortbread base is cooked and just starting to turn golden. Remove from the oven and leave to cool.

For the caramel, melt the butter and sugar together in a pan and heat until the butter just stops foaming. Add the condensed milk and continue to heat on a low temperature for 10–15 minutes, stirring constantly, until the mixture has turned golden. Meanwhile, place a small plate in the freezer for 5 minutes.

Test the mixture is firm enough by dripping a dot onto the cold plate from the freezer; it should form a firm caramel after a couple of minutes.

Pour and smooth the caramel over the shortbread while it is still hot. Leave to cool for at least 30 minutes.

For the chocolate layer, place the chocolate and cream in a microwaveable bowl and melt together. Start with a 1-minute burst in the microwave on high, then stir. Keep heating in 10-second bursts and stirring until it is nearly all melted. Use a rubber spatula to beat the mixture together to form a glossy, thick chocolate sauce.

Pour the chocolate over the caramel layer and smooth it.

Chill in the refrigerator for at least an hour before removing from the pan carefully and portioning. I find about a 5-cm/2-inch square is enough for me, but you might want yours larger! For afternoon tea, about a 2.5-cm/1-inch square is ample.

Rhubarb & custard slice

This slice is a take on a classic custard slice or mille-feuille, which brings back childhood memories for so many of us, especially when it's paired with the magical combination of rhubarb and custard. Use store-bought pastry; homemade puff pastry will shrink too much, and is too buttery and soft for this recipe.

PREPARE 30 MINUTES / COOK 45 MINUTES

150 g/5¼ oz. puff pastry
300 g/10½ oz. fresh rhubarb
vegetable oil, to coat
50 g/¼ cup Demerara sugar
200 ml/generous ¾ cup milk
100 ml/⅓ cup double/heavy cream
2 eggs
2 egg yolks
50 g/6 tablespoons plain/all-
　　purpose flour
1 teaspoon pure vanilla extract
100 g/½ cup caster/granulated
　　sugar

*non-stick 30 x 20-cm/12 x 8-inch
　brownie pan, lightly oiled and
　lined with baking parchment
baking sheet lined with baking
　parchment*

MAKES 10 SLICES

Preheat the oven to 180°C (350°F) Gas 4.

Roll out the pastry to a thickness of about 3 mm/⅛ inch and trim it to fit the base of the brownie pan. Use a fork to prick holes all over the base; this will stop the pastry rising too much. Bake in the preheated oven for 10–12 minutes until the top is golden and the pastry is cooked through. Don't worry too much if your pastry shrinks a little as you can trim the edges later. Remove from the oven and leave to cool. Leave the oven on.

Trim and cut the rhubarb into evenly-sized pieces, about 2 cm/¾ inch in length. Toss them with a little vegetable oil and then the Demerara sugar. Spread the rhubarb out on the lined baking sheet. Bake in the oven for 10–12 minutes, until they are just softened and cooked through.

In a heavy-bottomed saucepan, heat the milk and cream on a low heat, gently stirring, until just simmering, then take immediately off the heat. In a mixing bowl, whisk together the eggs, egg yolks, flour, vanilla and caster/granulated sugar to form a paste. Pour the hot milk and cream mixture into the mixing bowl, whisking constantly to combine into a thin custard.

Now return the custard to the saucepan and, carefully, on a low heat so as not to catch or burn it, whisk the custard over the heat until it is thickened and holding soft peaks.

Pour the thick custard over the pastry base and smooth it to make level. Carefully, place the rhubarb pieces on top of the custard; they should be half-submerged in the custard.

Place the brownie pan in the refrigerator for at least an hour before carefully removing and cutting the slice into 10 with a bread knife.

Bakewell slice

A slice or a tart or a pudding? Sweet fondant with a cherry on top, or just flaked/sliced almonds? There doesn't seem to be a Bakewell pudding that will please everyone. I like mine without the fondant and cherry as it's just too sweet for me. I'd rather build the sweetness into the three layers that no true Bakewell pudding can be without; a shortcrust base, a fruity layer and a frangipane filling.

PREPARE 30 MINUTES / COOK 50–60 MINUTES

PASTRY
150 g/generous 1 cup plain/
   all-purpose flour
100 g/7 tablespoons butter, chilled
50 g/¼ cup caster/granulated sugar
1 egg yolk

JAM/JELLY LAYER
150 g/generous ½ cup apricot
   jam/jelly

FRANGIPANE
120 g/1 stick butter, softened
120 g/generous ½ cup caster/
   granulated sugar
25 g/3 tablespoons plain/
   all-purpose flour
2 eggs
120 g/scant 1¼ cups ground
   almonds

GLAZE
grated zest and freshly squeezed
   juice of 1 lemon
20 g/2 tablespoons caster/
   granulated sugar
25 g/generous ¼ cup flaked/sliced
   almonds

*non-stick 30 x 20-cm/12 x 8-inch
   brownie pan, lightly oiled and
   lined with baking parchment*

MAKES 10

Preheat the oven to 160°C (325°F) Gas 3.

For the pastry, place the flour, cold butter and sugar into a food processor and pulse until they make a fine, dry mixture. Add the egg yolk and pulse again until it forms a ball of pastry.

Gently press the pastry into the base of the prepared brownie pan and place in the refrigerator for 30 minutes. Remove from the refrigerator and place in the preheated oven for 15–20 minutes, until the pastry is just starting to turn golden.

Remove from the oven and, whilst it is still warm, spread the apricot jam/jelly over the top of the pastry. The heat from the pastry will melt the jam, so spreading it is easy. Place in the refrigerator for 30 minutes to cool and set the jam.

For the frangipane, in a bowl, whisk the butter and sugar together for a few minutes to form a smooth, light-yellow, cream-like mixture. Keep whisking whilst slowly adding the flour and eggs until they are combined. Finally, add the ground almonds and fold them in to keep the mixture light and full of air.

Remove the brownie pan from the refrigerator, spoon the frangipane mixture over the apricot jam/jelly layer and smooth the top. To cook, place the brownie pan in the oven for 30 minutes. For the glaze, heat the lemon juice and zest, sugar and flaked/sliced almonds in a small saucepan. When the sugar has just dissolved, remove from the heat.

Remove briefly and spoon the glaze and almonds evenly over the top, then place back in the oven and bake for a further 5–10 minutes until the frangipane is cooked through and golden and the almond flakes/slices are toasted.

pictured page 52

Flapjacks

I used to make flapjacks as energy bars for when I was camping; they last well and are delicious as well as being full of energy. Add some chocolate, fruit or nuts... or all three to make them an indulgent treat, or bake a batch of the basic recipe for the week's lunch boxes.

PREPARE 10 MINUTES / COOK 20 MINUTES

500 g/5¼ cups rolled/
  old-fashioned oats
250 g/2¼ sticks butter
250 g/1¼ cups brown sugar
75 g/scant 4 tablespoons golden/
  light corn syrup

FRUIT AND NUT
100 g/1 cup chopped pecans
100 g/scant ¾ cup dried cranberries
30 g/1½ tablespoons maple syrup

CHOCOLATE
250 g/9 oz. milk chocolate

*non-stick 30 x 20-cm/12 x 8-inch
  brownie pan, lightly oiled and
  lined with baking parchment*

MAKES 12

Preheat the oven to 160°C (325°F) Gas 3.

Place the oats in a bowl. In a saucepan, heat the butter, brown sugar and golden/light corn syrup on a low heat until just melted. Stir together and pour over the rolled oats. Fold together, then press into the lined brownie pan.

Bake in the preheated oven for 20 minutes. Remove from the oven and allow to cool for 20 minutes before portioning.

Fruit and nut flapjacks

Before they are mixed with the melted butter, sugar and golden/light corn syrup, add the chopped pecans and cranberries to the rolled oats. Add the maple syrup to the melted mixture and stir to combine evenly. Pour into the mixing bowl containing the dry ingredients. Fold together, then press into the brownie pan. Bake as above.

Chocolate flapjacks

Line a baking sheet with baking parchment. Place 200 g/7 oz. of the chocolate into a microwaveable mixing bowl and microwave for 30 seconds on high, then stir. Keep heating in 15-second bursts and stirring until the chocolate is just melted. Add the remaining 50 g/2 oz. of chocolate and stir vigorously until it is combined and you have a thick chocolate sauce. Dip half, or more, of each baked flapjack into the chocolate. Shake off any excess and place them onto the lined baking sheet to set.

pictured page 53

White chocolate & strawberry tiffin

Delicious with coffee, these tiffins are fun to make with children.
Be inventive with swirly toppings and fillings.

PREPARE 20 MINUTES / COOK 10 MINUTES

250 g/2¼ sticks butter

120 g/generous ½ cup caster/
   granulated sugar

120 g/6 tablespoons golden/
   light corn syrup

200 g/7 oz. milk chocolate

100 g/¾ cup mixed dried fruit and
   nuts (almonds, sultanas/golden
   raisins, cherries)

100 g/1 cup fresh strawberries,
   chopped

450 g/1 lb. digestive biscuits/
   graham crackers, crushed

450 g/1 lb. white chocolate

*non-stick 30 x 20-cm/12 x 8-inch
   brownie pan, lightly oiled and
   lined with baking parchment*

MAKES 18

In a saucepan, place the butter, sugar and golden/light corn syrup. Warm on a low heat until melted and stir to mix together.

In a mixing bowl, grate 100 g/3½ oz. of the milk chocolate, then add the dried fruit and nuts, strawberries and crushed digestive biscuits/graham crackers. Pour in the melted butter, sugar and syrup mixture. Fold together until thoroughly mixed, then spoon into the lined brownie pan. Smooth the tiffin base to make it level, then place in the refrigerator for 15 minutes.

Melt the white chocolate by breaking it up and heating three-quarters of it in a microwave on high in a microwaveable bowl. Use the microwave in 10-second bursts, stirring the chocolate in-between until it is all melted. Now, add the remaining one-quarter and mix together to form a smooth, just-melted chocolate.

Remove the tiffin base from the refrigerator and pour the white chocolate over the top. Tilt the pan until the topping covers the tiffin base and is smooth and even.

Now melt the remaining milk chocolate in the same way (melting three-quarters of it, then adding the final one-quarter at the end). Pour the milk chocolate over the white chocolate in thin lines. Use a cocktail stick/toothpick to drag the milk chocolate over the surface to form patterns.

Return to the refrigerator for at least an hour, before removing and portioning with a hot knife.

Rocky road slice

Every kid's favourite! This mix of chocolate, nuts, fruit and marshmallows is hard to resist. Traditionally, dark/bittersweet chocolate is used, but I love it with a good-quality milk chocolate. To make a more adult rocky road, soak the sultanas/golden raisins in brandy overnight before using.

PREPARE 20 MINUTES

150 g/scant 1¼ cups whole roasted almonds or hazelnuts
150 g/3½ cups mini marshmallows
150 g/5 oz. fruit jelly sweets/candies, roughly chopped
100 g/¾ cup sultanas/golden raisins
100 g/¾ cup dried cranberries
750 g/1 lb. 10 oz. milk or dark/bittersweet chocolate
50 g/3½ tablespoons butter

non-stick 30 x 20-cm/12 x 8-inch brownie pan, lightly oiled and lined with baking parchment

MAKES 16

Into the lined brownie pan, spread the nuts, marshmallows, chopped sweets/candies, sultanas/golden raisins and cranberries to form a layer about 1.5 cm/⅝ inch deep.

Break the chocolate into small pieces and place, with the butter, in a microwaveable bowl. Melt the chocolate in the microwave in 30-second bursts on high, stirring between each burst. Stop heating when about two-thirds of the chocolate is melted. Stir the chocolate mixture until it is all melted and smooth. It should be a smooth, just pourable consistency; give it another burst in the microwave and stir if it is too thick.

Pour the chocolate mixture into the brownie pan, covering all of the ingredients press with a spatula to ensure it glues all of the dry ingredients, then together. Leave to set in the refrigerator for at least an hour.

Carefully remove the rocky road mixture from the pan by lifting the paper lining, then cut it into portions with a sharp knife, warmed in boiling water.

Rice crispy squares with cherry marshmallow

There's something slightly addictive about the sugary crunch of a rice crispy slice. They're easy and quick to make. I add fruit pieces to bring the sweetness down a bit – my favourites are glacé/candied cherries.

PREPARE 10 MINUTES / COOK 5 MINUTES

200 g/6 cups marshmallows
200 g/generous 8 cups puffed rice cereal
150 g/generous 1 cup glacé/candied cherries, roughly chopped

non-stick 30 x 20-cm/12 x 8-inch brownie pan, lined with baking parchment

MAKES 12

Place the marshmallows in a heavy-bottomed saucepan and heat on a low heat, stirring to ensure the marshmallows melt evenly and do not stick. Once the marshmallows are all melted, add the puffed rice and chopped cherries and stir to coat them evenly with melted marshmallow.

Spoon the mixture into the prepared brownie pan and level with a wet spoon. Place into the refrigerator to cool and set for at least an hour.

Remove from the refrigerator and cut into portions with a sharp bread knife.

Lemon & lime meringue tartlets

Surprisingly simple to make, with a little practice, these tartlets use a Sablé sweet pastry or Pâte sablée, which can be quickly made in a food processor, and an Italian meringue which you will need a thermometer for.

PREPARE 30 MINUTES / COOK 20 MINUTES

PASTRY
200 g/1½ cups plain/all-purpose flour
100 g/7 tablespoons butter, at room temperature
20 g/scant ¼ cup ground almonds
60 g/7 tablespoons icing/confectioners' sugar, plus extra for dusting
1 egg yolk

TARTLET FILLING
2 eggs
1 egg yolk
30 g/2½ tablespoons caster/granulated sugar
150 ml/²⁄₃ cup double/heavy cream
grated zest and freshly squeezed juice of 1 lemon
grated zest and freshly squeezed juice of 1 lime

MERINGUE
2 egg whites
½ teaspoon pure vanilla extract
75 g/6 tablespoons caster/granulated sugar

6 small fluted tartlet pans or rings
sugar thermometer
cook's blowtorch

MAKES 6 TARTLETS

pictured page 62

Preheat the oven to 160°C (325°F) Gas 3.

For the pastry, blitz the flour, butter and almonds together in a food processor before adding the icing/confectioners' sugar, then the egg yolk. Continue to blitz until it forms a ball. Roll out the pastry to a thickness of about 2 cm/¾ inch. Wrap it in some clingfilm/plastic wrap and place in the refrigerator for an hour to chill.

Once the pastry is chilled, divide into six and roll each of these out to a thickness of about 3 mm/⅛ inch (I dust the pastry with a little icing/confectioners' sugar to stop it sticking). Place the pastry into the small tartlet pans or rings, covering the base and sides. Place the tartlet bases in the refrigerator for a further 30 minutes to relax the gluten in the flour.

Prick the tartlet bases with a fork to stop them rising and bake in the oven for 10 minutes to 'set' the pastry; it should be just cooked but still pale.

For the tartlet filling, whisk the eggs, egg yolk, sugar, cream, and juice and zest of the lemon and lime together, before carefully pouring into the tartlet bases. Bake the filled bases for 7–9 minutes. Check after 7 minutes to see whether the mix has just set, it should still wobble a little when shaken.

To make the meringue, you will need a spotlessly clean mixing bowl (I wipe mine with a little vinegar, or lemon juice, to remove any oil which will stop the meringue from setting firm).

Whisk the egg whites and vanilla to soft peaks.

Next, make a sugar syrup. In a heavy-bottomed saucepan, add enough water to just cover the base, then add the sugar and heat until the mixture is boiling and the temperature reaches 115°C/240°F.

Now, while continuing to whisk the egg whites, pour the hot sugar syrup in a slow stream into the mixing bowl. Keep whisking until firm peaks are formed. Spoon or pipe the Italian meringue onto the tartlets and use a blowtorch to caramelize it. Serve as they are, or gently warmed for 10 minutes in a very low oven to make them extra special.

Individual jaffa tarts

Orange candy-coated, chocolate Jaffa sweets, were my favourite as a kid (and adult) in New Zealand. These tarts make use of that perfect mix of flavours that takes me back to my childhood.

PREPARE 20 MINUTES / COOK 30 MINUTES

PASTRY
200 g/1½ cups plain/all-purpose flour
100 g/7 tablespoons butter, at room temperature
20 g/scant ¼ cup ground almonds
60 g/7 tablespoons icing/confectioners' sugar, plus extra for dusting
1 egg yolk

ORANGE CURD
100 g/7 tablespoons butter
2 eggs
2 egg yolks
75 g/6 tablespoons caster/granulated sugar
100 ml/⅓ cup orange juice (about 1 large orange)
2 teaspoons grated orange zest

CHOCOLATE TOPPING
200 g/7 oz. dark/bittersweet chocolate

6 small tart pans or a muffin pan

MAKES 6

pictured page 63

Preheat the oven to 160°C (325°F) Gas 3.

For the pastry, in a food processor, blitz the flour, butter and almonds together, before adding the icing/confectioners' sugar, and then the egg yolk. Continue to blitz until it forms a ball. Roll out the pastry to a thickness of about 2 cm/¾ inch. Wrap it in some clingfilm/plastic wrap and place in the refrigerator for an hour to chill.

Once the pastry is chilled, divide into six and roll each of these out to a thickness of about 3 mm/⅛ inch (I dust the pastry with a little icing/confectioners' sugar to stop it sticking). Place the pastry into the small tart pans or muffin pan, covering the base and sides. Place the tart bases in the refrigerator for a further 30 minutes to relax the gluten in the flour.

Prick the tart bases with a fork to stop them rising and bake in the preheated oven for 12 minutes until the bases are just starting to turn golden. Remove from the oven and set aside to cool.

For the orange curd, soften the butter in a microwave for 30 seconds on high. Place the butter and all of the other curd ingredients in a microwaveable bowl and whisk hard to fully combine. Heat the bowl of ingredients in 30-second bursts in the microwave. Remove and whisk hard between each microwave burst. After four or five bursts the mixture should be hot and thickened, if not, reduce the times to 15 seconds and keep whisking between bursts. Once the mixture is thickened, pour it into the bases, leaving a little room to pour the chocolate layer on top. Place in the refrigerator for at least an hour to set.

For the chocolate topping, in the microwave, melt 150 g/5 oz. of the chocolate in a microwaveable bowl. Use the microwave in 15-second bursts until all of the chocolate is melted, before adding the remaining 50 g/2 oz. of chocolate and stirring to combine and temper the chocolate. Pour the tempered chocolate over the top of each tart forming a thin layer. To decorate, I use the back of a fork to form four lines on the chocolate.

Jam tarts

Let's not mess around making puff pastry for these lovely tarts. Grab some ready-made, all-butter puff pastry if you can get some. They take less than 20 minutes to make from scratch and the contrast of chewy baked jam against buttery pastry puts to shame many more complicated treats! These are a bit scruffy compared to shortcrust jam tarts but the texture of puff pastry with the jam is a must for me.

PREPARE 10 MINUTES / COOK 12 MINUTES

150 g/5 oz. puff pastry
   (ideally all-butter pastry)
plain/all-purpose flour, for dusting
1 egg
apricot jam/jelly
Strawberry and Elderflower
   Jam/Jelly (see page 141)
Bramble and Rose Jam/Jelly
   (see page 140)

*non-stick muffin pan or mini
   tart pans, dusted with flour*

MAKES 12

Preheat the oven to 180°C (360°F) Gas 4.

Roll out the puff pastry on a lightly floured surface to about 3 mm/⅛ inch thickness.

Use a cup or glass as a guide to cut rounds of pastry a little bigger than the muffin holes or mini tart pans.

Press the pastry rounds into the pan and use a fork to put lots of holes on the base (not the sides) to stop the pastry rising too much. Whisk the egg and brush the pastry with a little of the whisked egg.

Bake the pastry in the preheated oven for 5 minutes, then remove from the oven and fill each tart case with a generous dollop of jam/jelly. Use a mixture of jams/jellies to create a range of flavours.

Bake the jam-filled tarts for a further 7 minutes to finish. Leave to cool for 10 minutes before serving.

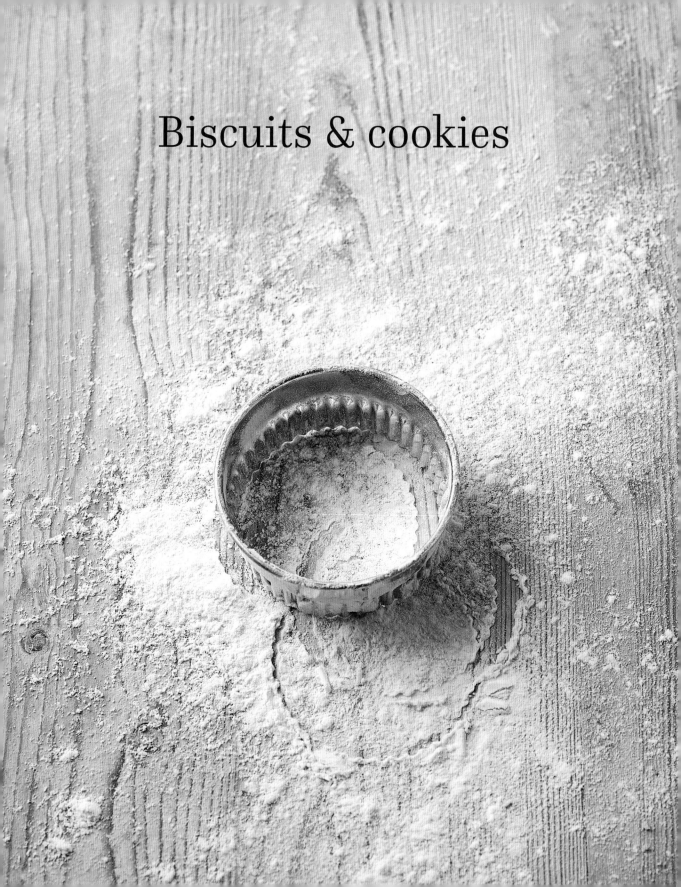

Biscuits & cookies

Shortbread

Wonderful to serve as a 'petticoat round' for afternoon tea. The traditional recipe for shortbread is a ratio of one sugar to two butter to three flour, by weight, so that is our basic recipe too, except we use a little cornflour/cornstarch to lighten it. Shortbread is simple to flavour, so I have included several of my favourite variations. Experiment and try your own ideas, I'd love to hear what you come up with!

PREPARE 15 MINUTES / COOK 12–15 MINUTES

BASIC SHORTBREAD
50 g/¼ cup caster/
   granulated sugar
100 g/¾ cup plain/
   all-purpose flour
50 g/½ cup cornflour/
   cornstarch
pinch of table salt
100 g/7 tablespoons
   butter, chilled

ALMOND SHORTBREAD
50 g/¼ cup caster/
   granulated sugar
50 g/6 tablespoons
   plain/all-purpose flour
50 g/½ cup ground
   almonds
50 g/½ cup cornflour/
   cornstarch
100 g/7 tablespoons
   butter, chilled
½ teaspoon almond
   extract

LAVENDER SHORTBREAD
50 g/¼ cup caster/
   granulated sugar
100 g/¾ cup plain/
   all-purpose flour

50 g/½ cup cornflour/
   cornstarch
100 g/7 tablespoons
   butter, chilled
1 teaspoon culinary
   lavender essence

EARL GREY
SHORTBREAD
2 teaspoons Earl Grey tea
   leaves
50 g/¼ cup caster/
   granulated sugar
100 g/¾ cup plain/
   all-purpose flour
50 g/½ cup cornflour/
   cornstarch
100 g/7 tablespoons
   butter, chilled
grated zest of 1 lemon

*2 x 15-cm/6-inch shortbread
   petticoat moulds
   (for petticoat shapes)*
*5-cm/2-inch cookie cutter
   (for cookies)*
*baking sheet lined with
   baking parchment
   (for cookies)*

MAKES 12 COOKIES OR
2 PETTICOAT ROUNDS

In a food processor, pulse all of the dry ingredients together. For the Earl Grey shortbread, do this with the tea leaves first, until the tea leaves are almost powder-like in size.

Now dice the butter into 5-mm/¼-inch pieces and add to the food processor, along with any flavouring. Pulse to form a crumbly texture. Do not over-mix.

Press the mixture into the two shortbread petticoat moulds.

Alternatively, if you are making cookies, press the mixture out between two sheets of baking parchment to about 5 mm/¼ inch thick. Cut into 5-cm/2-inch rounds using the cutter and place on the lined baking sheet. Use a fork to make holes on the top of the cookies; this stops them rising too much.

Chill for 30 minutes in the refrigerator before baking. Meanwhile, preheat the oven to 160°C (325°F) Gas 3.

Bake for approximately 15 minutes for the petticoat rounds or 12 minutes for individual cookies. Allow to cool in the moulds or on the baking sheet before moving, as they will be very crumbly and delicate while they are hot.

Serve with your favourite cup of tea.

Gingernuts

The classic afternoon tea cookie – easy to make and great for dunking.

PREPARE 10 MINUTES / COOK 20 MINUTES

100 g/7 tablespoons butter
50 g/¼ cup Demerera sugar
50 g/2½ tablespoons golden/
    light corn syrup
3 teaspoons finely grated fresh
    root ginger
200 g/1½ cups self-raising/
    self-rising flour
1 teaspoon ground ginger
1 teaspoon five-spice powder

*2 baking sheets lined with
    baking parchment*

MAKES 20

pictured page 80

Preheat the oven to 160°C (325°F) Gas 3.

In a heavy-bottomed saucepan, on a very low heat, melt the butter and add the sugar, golden/light corn syrup and grated fresh ginger to make a thick liquid. Stir to combine.

In a mixing bowl, combine the flour, ground ginger and five-spice powder, and mix thoroughly. Add the liquid ingredients and fold them all together to form a smooth mixture.

Use a dessertspoon to spoon balls of the mixture onto the lined baking sheets, allowing a 3-cm/1¼-inch gap between each one. Use a wet fork to press down on each one to flatten it slightly. Bake in the preheated oven for about 20 minutes until the cookies are just starting to turn golden, before removing them and allowing them to cool. Serve.

Stem ginger crunch cookies

A delicious crunchy ginger cookie. Try sticking two together with some buttercream for a 'ginger kiss' cookie.

PREPARE 10 MINUTES / COOK 15–20 MINUTES

100 g/7 tablespoons butter
30 g/1½ tablespoons golden/
    light corn syrup
25 g/2¼ tablespoons Demerara sugar
50 g/2 oz. stem ginger
150 g/generous 1 cup self-raising/
    self-rising flour
1 teaspoon ground ginger

*2 baking sheets lined with
    baking parchment*

MAKES 20

pictured page 81

Preheat the oven to 160°C (325°F) Gas 3.

In a heavy-bottomed pan, melt the butter, golden/light corn syrup and sugar on a low heat until just melted.

Finely chop the stem ginger into 3-mm/⅛-inch pieces.

In a mixing bowl, combine the finely chopped stem ginger, the flour and ground ginger, ensuring that the ginger pieces are separated and coated with flour. Add the melted ingredients and fold together to combine into a moist mixture.

Use a dessertspoon to spoon balls of the mixture onto the lined baking sheets. Bake in the preheated oven for 15–20 minutes until the cookies are just starting to turn golden. Remove from the oven and leave to cool.

Anzac biscuits

In New Zealand and Australia, Anzac biscuits/cookies are traditionally used as a fundraiser for returned servicemen, so they hold a special place in the hearts of everyone from either country. They are long-lasting, so they were made by wives and mothers during the Second World War and posted to servicemen. Today, no Australasian cafe would be without them, because they are absolutely delicious with a cup of tea (dunking required to soften them!).

PREPARE 10 MINUTES / COOK 15 MINUTES

100 g/³⁄₄ cup plain/all-purpose flour
200 g/1 cup caster/granulated sugar
75 g/1 cup desiccated/dried
   unsweetened shredded coconut
75 g/generous ³⁄₄ cup rolled/
   old-fashioned oats
150 g/1¹⁄₄ sticks butter
50 g/2¹⁄₂ tablespoons golden/
   light corn syrup
1 teaspoon bicarbonate of soda/
   baking soda
splash of boiling water

*2 baking sheets lined with
   baking parchment*

MAKES ABOUT 15

pictured page 84

Preheat the oven to 160°C (325°F) Gas 3.

Mix the flour, sugar, coconut and oats together in a large mixing bowl. Place the butter and golden/light corn syrup in a small saucepan and heat on a low heat until melted and combined.

In a bowl, combine the bicarbonate of soda/baking soda and a splash of boiling water to dissolve it. Stir, then pour into the saucepan with the butter and syrup. Add the liquid ingredients to the mixing bowl with the dry ingredients and stir to mix thoroughly.

Using a dessertspoon, form balls of the mixture and place on the lined baking sheets with a 2.5-cm/1-inch gap between each one.

Bake in the preheated oven for about 15 minutes, until golden. Remove from the oven and leave to cool and harden before removing them from the baking sheets.

Rose thins

Rose is one of my favourite flavours; it is fragrant, sweet and savoury. These cookie thins look so pretty decorated with rose petals.

PREPARE 15 MINUTES / COOK 10–12 MINUTES

THINS
100 g/7 tablespoons
    butter, softened
75 g/6 tablespoons caster/
    granulated sugar
1 egg
150 g/generous 1 cup
    plain/all-purpose flour,
    plus extra for dusting
1 teaspoon rose extract

CANDIED ROSE PETALS
30 fresh rose petals
    (from an old tea rose)
1 egg white
caster/superfine sugar

5-cm/2-inch cookie cutter
2 baking sheets lined with
    baking parchment

MAKES 20

pictured page 85

Preheat the oven to 160°C (325°F) Gas 3.

For the thins, in a mixing bowl, whisk all of the ingredients together to form a smooth mixture. Roll into a ball, wrap in clingfilm/plastic wrap and place in the refrigerator to chill for an hour.

On a lightly floured surface, roll the mixture out to a thickness of about 3 mm/⅛ inch. Using the cookie cutter, cut out rounds of cookie mixture.

Place the rounds onto the lined baking sheets. Bake in the preheated oven for 10–12 minutes, until the thins are just starting to turn golden.

Serve decorated with the candied rose petals.

Treacle oaties

An oatie makes a great snack for any time of the day. The treacle gives an almost liquorice-deep flavour, which I love.

PREPARE 10 MINUTES / COOK 10–12 MINUTES

100 g/¾ cup wholemeal/
    whole-wheat flour
1 teaspoon baking powder
100 g/1 cup rolled/old-fashioned oats
100 g/½ cup caster/granulated sugar
100 g/7 tablespoons butter
50 g/2 oz. treacle

2 baking sheets lined with
    baking parchment

MAKES 20

Preheat the oven to 160°C (325°F) Gas 3.

Put all of the dry ingredients in a mixing bowl and fold to combine.

Melt the butter and treacle together in a saucepan over a low heat. Pour the butter and treacle into the dry ingredients and fold together.

Place dessertspoon-sized rounds of the mixture onto the lined baking sheets. Bake in the preheated oven for 10–12 minutes until the cookies are just starting to turn golden.

Leave to cool on the baking sheets for 10 minutes before moving.

Venetian biscuits/cookies with milk chocolate cream

In Italy, Venetian biscuits/cookies are traditionally formed into an 'S' shape and hung from string or a rail. However, in the UK, they are made as a soft, buttery round biscuit/cookie, piped to form a 'rose', and two are stuck together with a generous layer of cream.

PREPARE 20 MINUTES / COOK 14 MINUTES

BISCUITS/COOKIES
250 g/generous 1¾ cups plain/
    all-purpose flour
125 g/generous ½ cup caster/
    granulated sugar
100 g/7 tablespoons butter
grated zest of 1 lemon
2 eggs
50 ml/3½ tablespoons milk

CHOCOLATE CREAM
100 g/3½ oz. milk chocolate,
    broken into small pieces
50 ml/3½ tablespoons double/
    heavy cream

*piping/pastry bag fitted
    with a rose nozzle/tip*
*2 baking sheets lined with
    baking parchment*

MAKES 12

For the biscuits/cookies, place the flour, sugar, butter and lemon zest into a food processor and pulse to combine. Add the eggs and pulse to form a smooth paste, then add enough of the milk to make a thick, creamy mixture, suitable for piping.

Spoon the mixture into the piping/pastry bag fitted with the rose nozzle/tip.

Pipe 24 rounds about 5 cm/2 inches in diameter onto the lined baking sheets.

Place in the preheated oven and bake for about 14 minutes, until the biscuits/cookies are just starting to turn golden. Remove from the oven and leave to cool on the baking sheets for 10 minutes then remove to a wire rack to cool completely.

For the chocolate cream, place the milk chocolate and cream in a microwaveable bowl and melt. Start with a 20-second burst in the microwave on high, then stir. Keep heating in 10-second bursts and stirring until it is melted. Beat the chocolate and cream together to form a smooth paste. Leave to cool.

Once the biscuits have cooled and the chocolate cream has thickened, place a teaspoonful of the chocolate cream on the flat side of one biscuit/cookie, stick it to the flat side of another, and give it a half-twist to spread the cream between the two halves. Repeat with the remaining cookies and chocolate cream.

Macaroons

Chewy macaroons are simple to make and feel as light as a feather. Whisk the egg mixture to firm peaks and add the sugar slowly to make a lighter, crunchy, meringue-like macaroon. Dip in melted chocolate for a special treat.

PREPARE 20 MINUTES / COOK 15–20 MINUTES

200 g/scant 3 cups shredded coconut
4 large/US extra-large egg whites
150 g/¾ cup caster/superfine sugar
1 teaspoon pure vanilla extract
1 teaspoon white wine vinegar
pinch of table salt

2 baking sheets lined with baking parchment

MAKES 20

Preheat the oven to 160°C (325°F) Gas 3.

Sprinkle the coconut onto a baking sheet and toast in the oven for 4–5 minutes, until it is just starting to turn golden. Remove from the oven and leave to cool.

In a mixing bowl, whisk the egg whites and sugar together until they are thoroughly mixed and they form soft peaks.

Next, fold in the toasted coconut, vanilla extract, vinegar and salt. Mix until they are fully combined.

Use a dessertspoon to spoon balls of the mixture onto the lined baking sheets. Wet the spoon and use it to slightly flatten the balls of mixture.

Bake in the preheated oven for 15–20 minutes until they are turning golden.

Leave to cool on the baking sheets for 10 minutes before transferring to a wire rack. Allow to cool completely before serving.

Fairy rings

These cookies are all about the icing, and are the ideal way to entertain children, as long as you don't mind a bit of a mess!

PREPARE 30 MINUTES / COOK 10 MINUTES

COOKIES

300 g/2¼ cups plain/all-purpose flour

150 g/¾ cup caster/granulated sugar

150 g/1¼ sticks butter, chilled and diced

1 egg

1 teaspoon pure vanilla extract

ICING

400 g/scant 3 cups Royal icing/confectioners' sugar

freshly squeezed juice of 3 limes

pink, blue, yellow, green icing colour pastes

decorations, such as sparkles and stars

1–1.5-cm/½-⅝ inch cookie cutter
7.5-cm/3-inch cookie cutter
4 small disposable piping/pastry bags
cocktail stick/toothpick

MAKES 25

For the cookies, place the flour, sugar and butter in a food processor and pulse until they are combined and crumbly. Add the egg and vanilla, then pulse again until a large ball of cookie dough is formed. Remove the dough from the food processor and chill in the refrigerator for at least 30 minutes.

Preheat the oven to 160°C (325°F) Gas 3.

Roll the dough out between two sheets of baking parchment to a thickness of about 5 mm/¼ inch. Remove the top sheet and carefully place the bottom sheet, with the dough on it, onto a baking sheet.

First, press out the centres using the small round cookie cutter, remove the centres and save. Now press out the outer rings using the large round cookie cutter, remove the excess dough and save. You should have enough dough left over to roll out and cut another batch of cookies while the first ones are baking. Bake the cookies in the preheated oven for 10–12 minutes, until they are just starting to turn golden.

Allow the cookies to cool on the baking sheet until they are cool enough to be moved, then place them onto a wire rack to cool completely. Place a clean sheet of baking parchment underneath the rack to catch any drips of icing. When the first batch are cooling, roll, shape and bake the second batch of cookies in the same way. For the icing, mix the Royal icing/confectioners' sugar with enough of the lime juice to allow it to just flow.

Divide the icing into four small bowls (I use tea cups) and add enough colour paste to each portion to colour one pink, one blue, one yellow and one green. Stir until each colour is thoroughly mixed in and the icing is smooth. Spoon into the small piping/pastry bags and snip off the ends.

Ice the base colour first. Pipe enough icing to cover the cookie and allow it to flow a little giving a smooth surface.

When it is just starting to dry, decorate with the other colours. Pipe dots and stripes. Use the tip of a toothpick to drag the dots to make stars or the stripes to make webs. Add sparkly decorations... have fun!

Dainties & patisserie

Lemon posset & raspberry verrine

Lemon posset is a fairly simple but always popular dessert. Paired with raspberry jelly/jello to make a pretty verrine, it's an afternoon tea delight. Try adding a little sherry to the mixture to make a posset for grown-ups.

PREPARE 30 MINUTES / COOK 10 MINUTES

LEMON POSSET
freshly squeezed juice of 1½ lemons
grated zest of 2 lemons
120 g/generous ½ cup caster/ granulated sugar
450 ml/scant 2 cups double/ heavy cream
30 ml/2 tablespoons sweet sherry or limoncello (optional)

TOPPING
200 g/1½ cups fresh raspberries
30 g/2½ tablespoons caster/ granulated sugar
freshly squeezed juice of ½ lemon
1 sheet gelatine
50 ml/3½ tablespoons water

4 jars or glasses, approx. 200-ml/7-fl. oz. capacity each

MAKES 4

For the topping, place the raspberries in a bowl with the sugar and lemon juice, and gently mix together. Leave at room temperature to infuse.

For the posset, in a small saucepan, heat the lemon juice, lemon zest and sugar until the sugar is dissolved. Take off the heat.

Place the cream into another saucepan and slowly warm until bubbles start to form on the sides of the pan. Stir gently but do not scrape the base of the pan. Take off the heat and add the optional alcohol, followed by the lemon and sugar mixture. Gently stir until everything is fully combined.

Pour the posset mixture into the jars or glasses, dividing it evenly. Cover with clingfilm/plastic wrap and place in the refrigerator for a couple of hours to set.

After a couple of hours, you can finish the topping. Place the gelatine leaf in cold water for 5 minutes to soften.

Strain the juice from the infused raspberries into a saucepan. Add the water and heat until it's just simmering. Take off the heat and add the softened gelatine sheet, then whisk until the leaf is fully dissolved. Add the raspberries to the jelly/jello mix and fold together before spooning carefully on top of the possets. Leave refrigerated for another 2 hours or longer until set.

These will keep for a few days in the refrigerator so it's a great dessert to prepare in advance.

Serve cool, but not fridge-cold.

Lavender mousse, blackberry & cinder toffee verrine

I won UK BBC MasterChef back in 2009 and this is a miniature version of the pudding I cooked in the final. The flavours work together beautifully, the sharp blackberries in the base, the summery aroma of the lavender mousse and the caramel crunch of cinder toffee (New Zealanders will know it as hokey pokey) which fizzes when you eat it with the blackberries.

PREPARE 30 MINUTES / COOK 5 MINUTES

BLACKBERRY COMPOTE
150 g/generous 1 cup blackberries
40 g/3¼ tablespoons caster/ granulated sugar
1 teaspoon white wine vinegar

LAVENDER MOUSSE
450 ml/scant 2 cups double/ heavy cream
50 g/generous ⅓ cup icing/ confectioners' sugar
lavender extract

CINDER TOFFEE
10 teaspoons caster/granulated sugar
4 teaspoons golden/light corn syrup
1 teaspoon bicarbonate of soda/ baking soda

4 verrine glasses, approx. 200-ml/7-fl. oz. capacity each

MAKES 4

For the blackberry compote, in a saucepan, gently heat the blackberries, sugar and vinegar until the blackberries just start to soften and break up. Mash them a little with a fork, then spoon them carefully into four verrine glasses. Place the glasses in the refrigerator for 30 minutes to chill.

For the lavender mousse, in a mixing bowl, whisk the cream, icing/ confectioners' sugar and a few drops of lavender extract together. Taste, you should be able to just taste the lavender but not overpoweringly so. Add a few drops more as needed but you don't want to be eating a soapy flavour, so go easy! Finish whisking until the cream is forming soft peaks. Carefully pipe or spoon into your verrine glasses on top of the compote. Tap the glasses on a flat surface to level the top of the cream. Refrigerate.

For the cinder toffee, cover a baking sheet with greaseproof paper and place it somewhere flat and stable. This should minimize the risk of spillage, as the cinder toffee will be very hot when poured onto the sheet.

In a deep, heavy-bottomed saucepan, just cover the base with a little water before adding the sugar and golden/light corn syrup. Have your bicarbonate of soda/baking soda to hand and a good whisk or silicone spatula. Heat on a medium heat until the mixture is turning a lovely caramel colour and smells of toffee. Add the bicarbonate of soda/baking soda and whisk carefully but quickly to combine (the mixture will foam up to about 4–5 times its previous volume). Pour the mixture out onto the greaseproof paper and leave to harden and cool.

To serve, firstly, break up the cinder toffee (I place it in a resealable sandwich bag and whack it on a flat surface), then sprinkle the shards over the tops of the verrines. Serve cool but not cold.

Sherry trifle verrines

A good sherry trifle is a work of art. Quality custard, sherry-drizzled sponge, freshly made fruit jelly/jello... I've made individual verrines, but the same recipe would also make a large trifle, perfect for a family get together.

PREPARE 60 MINUTES / COOK 10 MINUTES

JELLY/JELLO AND FRUIT
500 g/1 lb. 2 oz. mixed seasonal red berries
freshly squeezed juice of 2 lemons
100 g/½ cup caster/granulated sugar
3 sheets gelatine

SPONGE
½ Victoria Sandwich sponge (see page 25)
100 ml/⅓ cup Oloroso sherry

CUSTARD
200 ml/generous ¾ cup milk
100 ml/1/ cup double/heavy cream
2 eggs
2 egg yolks
50 g/6 tablespoons plain/all-purpose flour
1 teaspoon pure vanilla extract
100 g/½ cup caster/granulated sugar

ALMONDS
100 g/1¼ cups flaked/sliced almonds
vegetable oil

CREAM
600 ml/2½ cups double/heavy cream
100 g/¾ cup icing/confectioners' sugar
1 teaspoon pure vanilla extract

8 glasses or clear mugs approx. 200-ml/7-fl. oz. capacity each

MAKES 8

For the jelly/jello and fruit, place the berries in a bowl and pour the lemon juice and sugar over the fruit. Leave to macerate for at least 30 minutes.

Prepare the gelatine leaves by soaking them in cold water for 5 minutes. While they are softening, drain the liquid from the fruit into a small saucepan and heat gently. As soon as bubbles form on the sides of the pan, take it off the heat. Add the softened gelatine to the pan and whisk to dissolve the gelatine fully. Pour the jelly/jello back into the bowl with the fruit and fold to completely cover the fruit. Spoon the fruit and jelly/jello evenly into each of the glasses, and place in the refrigerator to chill and set.

For the sponge, drizzle the sponge with the sherry and leave for a few minutes to absorb fully. Break the sponge into 2.5-cm/1-inch pieces and place a layer of the sponge pieces into the glasses on top of the jelly/jello.

For the custard, heat the milk and cream in a heavy-bottomed pan over a low heat, gently stirring, until just simmering, then take immediately off the heat. In a mixing bowl, whisk together the eggs, egg yolks, flour, vanilla and sugar to form a paste. Pour the hot milk and cream mixture into the mixing bowl, continuously whisking to combine the mixture into a thin custard.

Now return the custard to the saucepan and carefully, on a low heat, so as not to catch or burn it, whisk the custard over the heat until it is thickened. Take off the heat and allow to cool for 30 minutes.

Pour the custard over the sponge pieces, tapping the glasses gently on the work surface to help the custard settle.

When you are ready to serve, toast the almonds and make the cream to top them. For the almonds, preheat the oven to 180°C (350°F) Gas 4. Toss the almonds in a little vegetable oil to coat, then place on a non-stick baking sheet and bake in the preheated oven for 5 minutes until golden. For the cream, whisk the cream, icing/confectioners' sugar and vanilla together until soft peaks are forming. Spoon the cream on top of the verrines, sprinkle with the toasted flaked almonds and serve.

Salted caramel tartlets

Salted caramel, done well, is a wonderful combination of sweet and bitter caramel, with a hint of saltiness which balances the flavours. These tartlets are just the right size for me and look great made in Madeleine moulds.

PREPARE 30 MINUTES / COOK 20 MINUTES

PASTRY
200 g/1½ cups plain/all-purpose flour
100 g/7 tablespoons butter, at room temperature, plus extra for the mould
30 g/⅓ cup unsweetened cocoa powder, plus extra for the mould
60 g/7 tablespoons icing/confectioners' sugar
2 egg yolks

CARAMEL
100 ml/⅓ cup water
100 g/½ cup caster/granulated sugar
100 ml/⅓ cup double/heavy cream
10 g/2 teaspoons table salt
sea salt, for sprinkling

non-stick 2 x 12-hole Madeleine moulds or 1 x 24-hole metal Madeleine mould (or similar)

MAKES 24

For the pastry, blitz the flour, butter and cocoa powder together in a food processor, before adding the icing/confectioners' sugar, followed by 1 egg yolk. Continue to blitz until it forms a ball of dough.

Roll out the pastry to a thickness of about 2 cm/¾ inch. Wrap it in some clingfilm/plastic wrap and place in the refrigerator for an hour to chill.

Lightly butter the Madeleine moulds, then dust with cocoa powder and place in the refrigerator for at least 30 minutes to chill. Meanwhile, preheat the oven to 160°C (325°F) Gas 3.

Once the pastry is chilled, break off dessertspoon-sized pieces. Using a spoon, press the pastry into the Madeleine moulds to a thickness of about 3 mm/⅛ inch, leaving a smooth depression. Place the moulds in the refrigerator for a further 30 minutes to relax the gluten in the flour.

Prick the tartlet bases with a fork to stop them rising and then bake in the preheated oven for 10 minutes to 'set' the pastry.

Whisk the remaining egg yolk and brush the tartlet bases with it before returning them to the oven for a further 3 minutes to glaze them.

For the caramel, in a heavy-bottomed saucepan, heat the water and sugar over a medium heat. The sugar should all melt into the water; swirl it carefully to ensure this happens, otherwise it can seize and be lumpy.

As the sugar mixture continues to heat, the water will boil off and the sugar will start to caramelize. When the caramel is brown (it should smell like toffee), take it off the heat and add the cream (be careful as the caramel is very hot). Stir to combine into a thick caramel syrup. If lumps have formed that stirring won't clear, then place the pan back on a low heat until they are all dissolved. Add the table salt and whisk to combine.

Pour the caramel into the pastry shapes and place in the refrigerator for at least 30 minutes to chill and set.

Serve with a tiny pinch of sea salt on top of the caramel.

pictured page 102

Crème brûlée spoons

My favourite dessert is a crème brûlée, and these spoon-sized versions are just the perfect accompaniment to an afternoon tea. I put a little lemon juice in my crème brûlée which reduces the sweetness and helps them to set.

PREPARE 10 MINUTES / COOK 10 MINUTES

150 ml/²/₃ cup double/heavy cream
1 egg
1 egg yolk
50 g/¼ cup caster/granulated sugar, plus extra for topping
freshly squeezed juice of ½ lemon

12 deep china spoons
cook's blowtorch

MAKES 12

In a heavy-bottomed saucepan, heat the cream over a low heat, gently stirring, until it is just simmering, then take it immediately off the heat.

In a mixing bowl, whisk together the egg, egg yolk and sugar to form a paste. Pour the hot cream into the mixing bowl, continuously whisking to combine into a custard, before finally adding the lemon juice.

Now return the custard to the saucepan and carefully, on a low heat, so as not to catch or burn it, whisk the custard over the heat until it is thickened.

Spoon the custard evenly into the serving spoons while it is hot and tap them to level the custard and remove any air bubbles. Place the serving spoons in the refrigerator for at least an hour to chill.

To serve, sprinkle enough caster/granulated sugar over each spoonful of custard to cover it. Using a blowtorch, caramelize the sugar, forming a hard surface of caramel on top.

pictured page 103

Macarons

Once you have mastered macarons, you will be the envy of your foodie friends. You can play with colours and flavours for the meringue and the buttercream, my favourite is lime and ginger. It's a myth that they're difficult to make, this recipe will give you consistent results every time, but, as with so many baking recipes, the need for fresh eggs is critical here.

PREPARE 25 MINUTES / COOK 15 MINUTES

MACARONS
a squeeze of lemon juice
2 egg whites
**60 g/5 tablespoons caster/
    superfine sugar**
**100 g/3/4 cup icing/confectioners'
    sugar**
100 g/1 cup ground almonds
**your choice of food colouring paste
    and dry flavours, such as lime zest**

BUTTERCREAM
**50 g/3 1/2 tablespoons butter,
    softened**
**100 g/3/4 cup cups icing/
    confectioners' sugar**
1 teaspoon warm water
**your choice of food colouring and
    flavours**

disposable piping/pastry bag
*2 baking sheets lined with
    baking parchment*

MAKES 24 PAIRS

Preheat the oven to 120°C (250°F) Gas 1/2.

For the macarons, wipe out your food mixer bowl with a good squeeze of lemon juice and a dry paper towel.

Add the egg whites and, using a balloon whisk, start whisking until soft peaks form. Add the caster/superfine sugar, one-third at a time, whisking until firm peaks form each time. When all of the sugar has been whisked in and dissolved, you will have a firm, uncooked meringue mixture.

Add the icing/confectioners' sugar and ground almonds, and fold into the meringue mixture. At this stage you can add a few drops of colouring and flavours, if desired.

Spoon the meringue mix into the piping/pastry bag and snip off the end. Pipe 5-cm/2-inch rounds onto the lined baking sheets. Tap the sheets to remove any bubbles and leave to settle for 5 minutes.

Bake the macarons for 15 minutes, opening the door after 10 minutes to let any excess moisture out. They should have formed crisp outer shells. Remove from the oven and leave to cool fully on the baking sheets before moving.

For the buttercream, in a mixing bowl, whisk together the butter, icing/confectioners' sugar and a few drops of colouring, if desired. Add the warm water to make the buttercream lighter.

Add 1/2 teaspoon of the buttercream to the flat side of a macaron shell and stick another macaron shell to it by gently twisting together. Repeat with the remaining shells.

Profiteroles

Profiteroles, or filled choux pastries, were one of my first 'wow' moments when learning to cook. To take a few simple ingredients and make something so light and tasty was a revelation. The pastry is extremely versatile – this recipe is for simple filled choux buns or profiteroles, but you can also make flavoured choux eclairs, like my Camp Coffee and Caramel Eclairs on page 111, or my savoury Cheese Choux on page 137.

PREPARE 25 MINUTES / COOK 15 MINUTES

CHOUX PASTRY
75 g/½ cup strong bread flour
150 ml/⅔ cup water
75 g/5 tablespoons butter
2 eggs

FILLING
300 ml/1¼ cups double/heavy cream
50 g/6 tablespoons icing/ confectioners' sugar
1 teaspoon pure vanilla extract

TO DECORATE
melted chocolate or icing/ confectioners' sugar

2 baking sheet lined with baking parchment

MAKES 25

Preheat the oven to 200°C (400°F) Gas 6.

For the choux pastry, place the flour in a stand mixer and, using a pastry attachment, start mixing slowly. In a large saucepan, heat the water and butter and bring to the boil. Take off the boil and immediately pour the hot mixture over the flour in the mixer. Beat the hot mixture using a medium speed, until it is all combined, then, one at a time, add the eggs and beat until the pastry is smooth.

Using a teaspoon, form balls of the choux pastry and place on the lined baking sheets with a 2.5-cm/1-inch gap between each one. Bake in the preheated oven for about 15 minutes, until golden.

Remove from the oven and place on a wire rack to cool, pricking each choux ball with a small knife as you place them on the rack (the hole will allow steam to escape and stop them becoming soggy).

For the filling, in a mixing bowl, whip the cream, icing/confectioners' sugar and vanilla together until the mixture forms peaks. Spoon the whipped cream into a piping/pastry bag. Just before serving, snip off the end of the bag and squirt a blob of cream into the centre of each choux bun through the hole you made to allow the steam to escape.

Cover the tops of the profiteroles with melted chocolate to decorate. Alternatively, dust with a little icing/confectioners' sugar. Serve immediately; 4 or 5 per person.

Camp coffee & caramel éclairs

Camp Coffee is often thought of as a coffee substitute developed during the Great War; it was, in fact, produced for nearly 50 years before this. It is a mixture of a small amount of coffee essence (caffeine-free) and chicory essence. If you can't find any to buy (I use the internet), then strong coffee, made with instant coffee powder, is a decent substitute.

PREPARE 30 MINUTES / COOK 30 MINUTES

CHOUX PASTRY
75 g/½ cup strong bread flour
150 ml/⅔ cup water
75 g/5 tablespoons butter
2 eggs

CARAMEL
100 ml/⅓ cup water
100 g/½ cup caster/superfine sugar
50 ml/3½ tablespoons double/
   heavy cream

CAMP COFFEE CREAM
300 ml/1¼ cups double/heavy
   cream
50 g/6 tablespoons icing/
   confectioners' sugar
1 teaspoon Camp Coffee
   (or use strong instant coffee)

*baking sheet lined with
   baking parchment*
*2 piping/pastry bags fitted with
   large round nozzles/tips*

MAKES 12

Preheat the oven to 200°C (400°F) Gas 6.

For the choux pastry, place the flour in a stand mixer fitted with a pastry attachment and start mixing slowly.

In a large saucepan, heat the water and butter and bring to the boil. Take off the boil and immediately pour the hot mixture over the flour in the mixer. Beat the hot mixture using a medium speed, until it is all combined. Then, one at a time, add the eggs, while continuing to beat, until the pastry is smooth.

Using one of the piping/pastry bags, make sausage shapes of pastry on the lined baking sheet, leaving a clear 2.5-cm/1-inch gap between them.

Bake in the preheated oven for about 15 minutes until golden.

Remove from the oven and place on a wire rack to cool. Prick each éclair with a small knife before placing on the rack (the hole will allow steam to escape and stop them becoming soggy).

For the caramel, heat the water and sugar in a heavy-bottomed saucepan over a medium heat. The sugar should all melt into the water; swirl it carefully to ensure this happens, otherwise it can seize and be lumpy.

As the sugar mixture continues to heat, the water will boil off and the sugar will start to caramelise. When the caramel is brown (it should smell like toffee), take it off the heat and add the cream (be careful, it's very hot). Stir to combine into a thick caramel syrup. If lumps have formed that stirring won't clear, place the pan back on a low heat until they are all dissolved.

For the camp coffee cream, whip the cream, icing/confectioners' sugar and Camp Coffee together until soft peaks form. Spoon the cream into the second piping/pastry bag. Use a sharp bread knife to cut each éclair in half lengthways and pipe the coffee cream into the middle generously. Drizzle the top of the éclairs with the caramel.

Raspberry meringue kisses

Dehydrated raspberries are a staple in my kitchen as they have a lovely sharpness that offsets sweet meringue and cream perfectly.

PREPARE 20 MINUTES / COOK 45 MINUTES

RASPBERRIES
200 g/1½ cups raspberries
freshly squeezed juice of ½ lemon
or
40 g/1½ oz. dehydrated raspberry powder

MERINGUES
200 g/1 cup caster/superfine sugar
100 g/½ cup egg whites (approx. 3 large/US extra-large eggs)

BUTTERCREAM
50 g/3½ tablespoons butter, softened
100 g/¾ cup icing/confectioners' sugar
1 teaspoon pure vanilla extract

piping/pastry bag
2 baking sheets lined with baking parchment

MAKES 12

For the raspberries (if using fresh raspberries), preheat the oven to 90°C (195°F). Place a sheet of baking parchment over a wire rack.

Spread the raspberries over the baking parchment and sprinkle with the lemon juice. Place in the preheated oven and leave in the oven overnight, or for at least 8 hours. Once dried, blitz the raspberries in a food processor until they form a fine powder, then pass them through a sieve/strainer.

For the meringues, preheat the oven to 200°C (400°F) Gas 6. Ensure the bowl you use is perfectly clean. Sprinkle the sugar over a non-stick baking sheet and place into the preheated oven. At the same time, place the egg whites into a stand mixer fitted with a balloon whisk (or use a mixing bowl and a hand-held electric whisk) and start mixing until stiff peaks form; this will take 5–8 minutes. Remove the, now hot, sugar from the oven and turn the oven down to 100°C (210°F).

Add about one-quarter of the sugar to the egg white mix. Whisk for a couple of minutes, then repeat until all of the sugar has been combined. Whisk for another 5 minutes, checking that the mixture is fully combined and that no graininess remains. Finally, add about three-quarters of the raspberry powder and fold together, but leave some patterns in the mixture.

Spoon the meringue mixture into the piping/pastry bag and snip off the tip. Pipe the meringue mixture onto the lined baking sheets, making about 24–26 5-cm/2-inch kisses. Bake in the preheated oven for 45 minutes. Check the outer layer of meringue has fully cooked and is crispy; continue cooking in 10-minute intervals if not. Switch the oven off and leave the meringues to cool in the oven for at least 30 minutes. Store the meringues in an airtight container until you are ready to serve.

For the buttercream, in a mixing bowl, whisk the butter and icing/confectioners' sugar together to form a smooth cream. Add the vanilla and 4–5 teaspoons of water. Whisk until a smooth, light buttercream is made. To serve, place a teaspoon of the buttercream onto the flat side of one meringue and stick it to the flat side of another. Sprinkle a little remaining raspberry powder over the top to decorate.

Chocolate tea cakes

Chocolate teacakes are personal favourites of mine. I like to drizzle the chocolate over the top but not completely cover the marshmallow and jam.

PREPARE 25 MINUTES / COOK 45 MINUTES

MARSHMALLOWS
7 g/¼ oz. powdered gelatine
200 g/1 cup caster/granulated sugar
1 teaspoon pure vanilla extract

COOKIES
100 g/7 tablespoons butter
50 g/¼ cup Demerara sugar
150 g/generous 1 cup plain/
    all-purpose flour

FILLING
50 g/2 oz. Strawberry and
    Elderflower Jam/Jelly
    (see page 141)

COATING
250 g/9 oz. dark/bittersweet
    chocolate

12 5-cm/2-inch half-sphere
    silicone moulds, lightly oiled
2 baking sheets lined with
    baking parchment
6-cm/2½-inch round
    cookie cutter

MAKES 12

For the marshmallows, soak the gelatine in 100 ml/⅓ cup of cold water for at least 5 minutes until softened.

Cover the bottom of a heavy-bottomed saucepan with a little water and add the sugar. Heat until it foams, then continue to heat on very low until a temperature of 113°C/236°F is reached, or until a drop from the mixture forms a soft ball when dripped into a glass of cold water. Using a stand mixer, carefully whisk the water and gelatine whilst slowly adding the hot sugar syrup in a thin stream. Once all of the sugar syrup is added, add the vanilla extract, then whisk for 15 minutes until the mixture is beginning to cool.

Spoon the marshmallow mixture into the prepared half-sphere moulds. Dip a spatula in water, then clean and level the tops. Place the marshmallows in the freezer until set and firm.

For the cookies, preheat the oven to 160°C (325°F) Gas 3.

Melt the butter and sugar together in the microwave for 1 minute on high then fold in the flour. Knead the mixture a little before rolling out onto one of the lined baking sheets. Cut out 12 6-cm/2½-inch rounds with the cookie cutter and remove. Bake in the preheated oven for 20 minutes until they are just starting to turn golden. Leave to cool and harden.

Place a cookie on a wire rack over a piece of baking parchment. Onto the middle of the cookie, add a teaspoon of jam/jelly. Remove a marshmallow from the mould and place, flat-side down, on the cookie. Repeat.

Place 200 g/7 oz. of the chocolate in a microwaveable bowl and melt. Start with a 15-second burst in the microwave on high, then stir. Keep heating in 15-second bursts and stirring until it is melted. Add the remaining 50 g/2 oz. of chocolate and, using a rubber spatula, beat the chocolate together to combine and temper the chocolate. Drizzle the chocolate over the marshmallows and cookies. Leave to drip for a few minutes before placing on the second lined baking sheet. Place in a refrigerator to set the chocolate.

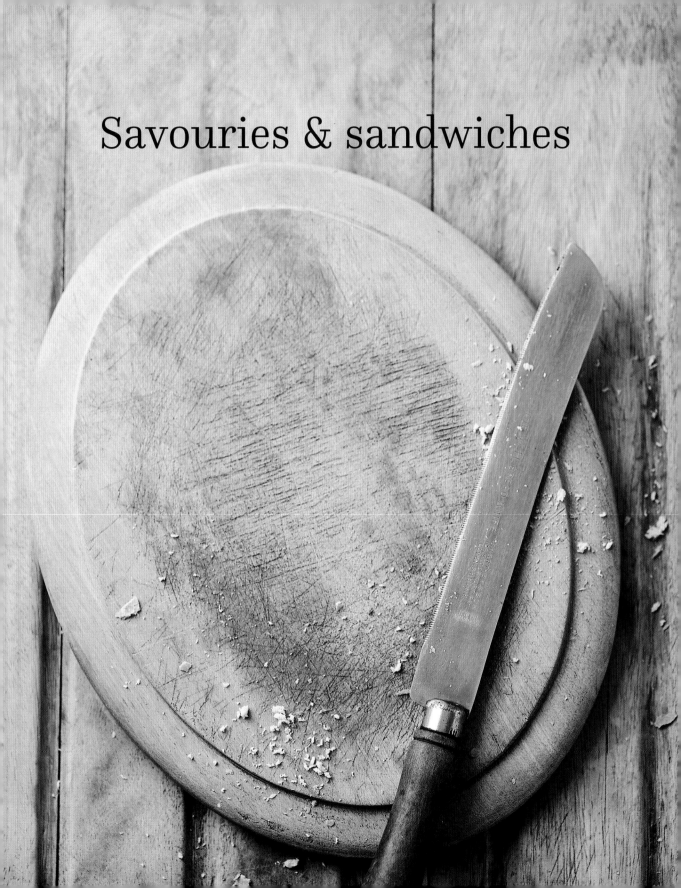

Savouries & sandwiches

Milk bread

Few things are as satisfying as making your own bread. This recipe makes a soft loaf of bread ideal for slicing and making sandwiches, and it uses milk and butter to create its unique flavour.

PREPARE 60 MINUTES / COOK 45 MINUTES

200 ml/generous ¾ cup milk

2 teaspoons caster/granulated sugar

75 g/5 tablespoons butter

100 ml/⅓ cup boiling water

15 g/1 tablespoon fresh yeast or 7 g/¼ oz. active dried yeast

500 g/generous 3½ cups strong bread flour (white or wholemeal/ whole-wheat)

2 teaspoons table salt

vegetable oil, for coating

non-stick 900-g/2-lb loaf pan, lightly oiled

MAKES 1 LOAF

Place the milk, sugar, butter and boiling water into the bowl of a stand mixer, then the yeast. Add the flour on top of the water and leave for 15 minutes to activate the yeast. It should be just starting to bubble around the edges of the flour.

Place the mixer bowl into the mixer and fit the dough hook. Start mixing on the lowest speed for a few minutes. Add the salt and continue mixing for another 5–10 minutes, until the dough is forming a ball and is smooth in appearance.

Scrape the dough off the dough hook and away from the sides of the bowl. Drizzle a little vegetable oil over the dough to just coat it in oil.

Cover the top of the bowl with a piece of clingfilm/plastic wrap and leave for 30–45 minutes in a warm place, until the dough has doubled in size.

Place the dough in the oiled loaf pan. Oil your fingers and press the dough carefully into the corners, then gently tap the loaf pan on the work surface to fill any gaps. The loaf pan should be just over half full.

Leave the dough to rise again in a warm place until it has completely filled the loaf pan and is starting to rise above the top. Meanwhile, preheat the oven to 160°C (325°F) Gas 3.

Bake in the preheated oven for 45 minutes, until just turning golden brown and a little crispy. Remove from the oven and rest in the pan for 5 minutes before turning out onto a wire rack.

Slice once it has fully cooled.

CLASSIC
SANDWICHES

Cucumber & mint

One of the most popular sandwiches in the cafe is cucumber and mint. I wasn't at all sure of it as a flavour combination until I tried it; it really works. I have lightly salted the cucumber slices in this recipe using salt water.

PREPARE 10 MINUTES

**6 slices of soft Milk Bread
(see page 118)**
whipped butter, for spreading
1 tablespoon table salt
1 cucumber
a small bunch of fresh mint
100 ml/⅓ cup crème fraîche

MAKES 12

Lay out the slices of bread on a bread board. Spread whipped butter evenly and thinly on the slices to seal the bread.

In a mixing bowl, add a few cm/inches of cold water and the table salt, then whisk to dissolve the salt. Taste the water to check it has a hint of saltiness.

Peel and thinly slice the cucumber. Place the slices into the salted water for a few minutes, then remove them and set aside. Finely chop the mint and whisk into the crème fraîche to make a minty cream.

Spread the mint cream on three of the slices of buttered bread. Lay the cucumber slices on top of the cream and cover with the second slices of buttered bread. Cut the edges off the sandwiches, then cut them into four triangles. Serve.

Smoked salmon & dill mayonnaise

Dill and smoked salmon are a classic combination because they are perfectly balanced. Try using hot smoked salmon for a tasty alternative.

PREPARE 10 MINUTES

**6 slices of soft Milk Bread
(see page 118)**
whipped butter, for spreading
50 ml/3½ tablespoons mayonnaise
**a small bunch of fresh dill,
picked and finely chopped**
**200 g/7 oz. smoked salmon,
thinly sliced**

MAKES 12

Lay out the slices of bread on a bread board. Spread whipped butter evenly and thinly on the slices to seal the bread.

Spread the mayonnaise generously on three of the slices of buttered bread, then sprinkle with finely chopped dill.

Lay slices of smoked salmon, two layers thick, over the dill and mayonnaise, and cover with the second slices of buttered bread.

Cut the edges off the sandwiches, then cut each into four triangles. Serve.

Aubergine/eggplant & mayonnaise

Aubergine/eggplant goes particularly well with smoky flavours, as in this recipe.

PREPARE 10 MINUTES/ COOK 10 MINUTES

6 slices of soft Milk Bread
   (see page 118)
whipped butter, for spreading
1 large aubergine/eggplant
table salt
vegetable oil, for drizzling
100 ml/⅓ cup mayonnaise
3 teaspoons smoked paprika

MAKES 12

Lay out the slices of bread on a bread board. Spread whipped butter evenly and thinly on the slices to seal the bread.

Cut the aubergine/eggplant lengthways into eight thin slices and lightly season with salt. Place into a large, preheated, dry non-stick frying pan/skillet. Heat on high and allow the aubergine/eggplant to cook and char a little on both sides. Drizzle a little vegetable oil over the aubergine/eggplant and fry for a couple of minutes. Leave to cool.

In a mixing bowl, mix together the mayonnaise and smoked paprika.

Spread the mayonnaise evenly on three of the slices of buttered bread. Slice the cooked aubergine/eggplant into 2.5-cm/1-inch strips and place these on the mayonnaise, overlapping them to make a generous layer of aubergine/eggplant. Cover with the second slices of buttered bread. Cut the edges off the sandwiches, then cut each into four triangles. Serve.

Hummus and rocket/arugula

I've used rocket/arugula leaves to add a little heat and freshness to the hummus.

PREPARE 10 MINUTES

6 slices of soft Milk Bread
   (see page 118)
whipped butter,
   for spreading
bag of wild rocket/
   arugula, washed

HUMMUS
200 g/1½ cups drained
   cooked chickpeas/
   garbanzo beans
grated zest and freshly
   squeezed juice of
   1 lemon

50 g/2 oz. tahini
1 garlic clove
1 teaspoon ground
   cumin
1 teaspoon smoked
   paprika
½ teaspoon table salt
a splash of extra-virgin
   olive oil

MAKES 12

For the hummus, put all of the ingredients into a small food processor and blitz for about a minute, until it forms a rough paste. Add a little more oil, if needed, to thin the mixture. Leave for at least 30 minutes for the flavours to infuse before serving.

Lay out the slices of bread on a bread board. Spread whipped butter evenly and thinly on the slices to seal the bread.

Spread the hummus generously on three of the slices of bread, then cover each with at least three layers of washed rocket/arugula leaves. Cover with the second slices of buttered bread. Cut the edges off the sandwiches, then cut each into four triangles. Serve.

Beef & horseradish

A traditional roast beef sandwich should be served rare, but it's what you like that counts, so cook it your way. This sandwich is quite often my lunch on a Monday, using up the leftovers from the Sunday roast... I think I look forward to them as much as the roast itself!

PREPARE 10 MINUTES

6 slices of soft Milk Bread
   (see page 118)
whipped butter, for spreading
100 g/3½ oz. horseradish sauce
250 g/9 oz. thinly sliced cold
   roast beef

MAKES 12

Lay out the slices of bread on a bread board. Spread whipped butter evenly and thinly on the slices to seal the bread.

Spread a thin layer of horseradish sauce on three of the slices of buttered bread (or more generously if you like it extra spicy).

Lay slices of the beef on top, at least three thin slices deep, in my opinion. Cover with the second slices of buttered bread.

Cut the edges off the sandwiches, then cut each into four triangles. Serve.

Egg & cress

Egg sandwiches remind my wife, Amanda, of childhood picnics on the beach. She remembers them as slightly warm, squashed and wrapped in foil. Despite this, she still remembers them fondly! Seven minutes in boiling water (for a room temperature egg) gives a just-hard-boiled/-cooked egg.

PREPARE 10 MINUTES

6 slices of soft Milk Bread
   (see page 118)
whipped butter, for spreading
2 cold hard-boiled/hard-cooked eggs
a pinch of ground white pepper
a pinch of table salt
30 g/1 oz. cress

MAKES 18

Lay out the slices of bread on a bread board. Spread whipped butter evenly and thinly on the slices to seal the bread.

Peel the eggs and place in a mixing bowl. Mash the eggs with a fork, adding a generous pinch of white pepper and salt.

Spread the mashed egg mixture on three of the slices of buttered bread, then sprinkle with an even covering of fresh cress. Cover with the second slices of buttered bread. Cut the edges off the sandwiches, then cut each into six fingers. Serve.

Ham & mustard

The simplicity of this sandwich means the ingredients need to be of the best quality. A good cured ham is vastly different from a cheap pressed ham. I prefer my ham sliced thickly, but for a proper afternoon tea it should be wafer thin.

PREPARE 10 MINUTES

6 slices of soft Milk Bread
   (see page 118)
whipped butter, for spreading
English mustard, to taste
300 g/10½ oz. cured ham,
   thinly sliced

MAKES 12

Lay out the slices of bread on a bread board. Spread whipped butter evenly and thinly on the slices to seal the bread.

Spread about half a teaspoon of English mustard (or to taste) on three of the slices of bread. Divide the ham between the three slices and then cover each with the second slices of buttered bread.

Cut the edges off the sandwiches, then cut each into four triangles. Serve.

Coronation chicken

Originally known as Jubilee Chicken for George V's 25th Jubilee, the classic coronation chicken was re-invented for post-war Britain in 1953 to celebrate the Queen's coronation. This classic dish was made with mayonnaise and curry powder; here we use a similar mix but use some classic, fresh, individual spices.

PREPARE 10 MINUTES

6 slices of soft Milk Bread
   (see page 118)
whipped butter, for spreading
1 teaspoon coriander seeds
½ teaspoon ground turmeric
½ teaspoon chilli/chili powder
½ teaspoon fenugreek powder
a pinch of ground cumin
150 ml/⅔ cup fresh mayonnaise
300 g/10½ oz. cold cooked chicken,
   finely diced

MAKES 12

Lay out the slices of bread on a bread board. Spread whipped butter evenly and thinly on the slices to seal the bread.

In a dry frying pan/skillet, heat the coriander seeds until they start to crack and pop. Take the pan off the heat and add all the other spices, mixing with a wooden spoon and using the residual heat to cook them. Crush the coriander seeds with the back of the wooden spoon.

Place the mayonnaise into a mixing bowl and add the spices. Mix to combine evenly, then add the chicken. Fold the meat through the mixture to coat it evenly. Spread the coronation chicken generously on three of the slices of bread and cover each with the second slices of buttered bread. Cut the edges off the sandwiches, then cut each into four triangles. Serve.

Welsh rarebit

Yes, it's cheese on toast, but it's the best cheese on toast you can make. My Welsh rarebit has a hot, cheesy, ale-infused béchamel sauce under a crispy, grilled/broiled cheese topping, served on crispy toasts!

PREPARE 30 MINUTES / COOK 10–12 MINUTES

BÉCHAMEL
40 g/3 tablespoons butter
25 g/3 tablespoons plain/
   all-purpose flour
100 ml/⅓ cup milk
300 ml/1¼ cups ale
Worcestershire sauce
1 teaspoon English mustard
150 g/2 cups grated/shredded
   Parmesan cheese
150 g/1⅔ cups grated/shredded
   Cheddar cheese
table salt, to taste

TOAST
1 ciabatta roll
vegetable oil

TOPPING
50 g/generous ½ cup grated/
   shredded Parmesan cheese
50 g/½ cup grated/shredded
   Cheddar cheese

SERVES 12

For the béchamel, in a small saucepan, heat the butter and flour over a medium heat. Leave on the heat until the butter is foaming, then whisk the mixture to a smooth paste. With the pan still on the heat, add all the milk and whisk until thoroughly combined. Slowly, add the ale, whisking to make a light brown sauce with a cream-like consistency.

Add a couple of glugs of Worcestershire sauce and the mustard before adding the grated/shredded cheeses. Whisk over a low heat until a cheesy, ale-infused, béchamel sauce is formed. Add a generous pinch of salt to taste. Add a little more Worcestershire sauce and mustard if you prefer a stronger flavour.

Your sauce is now made. It is easier to use when chilled, so make it in advance if you can and refrigerate. The sauce will keep for several days in the refrigerator. The recipe makes more than you need for one batch of Welsh Rarebit so you can freeze what you won't use this time.

Preheat the oven to 160°C (325°F) Gas 3.

For the toast, thinly slice a ciabatta roll and drizzle with a little oil. Place on a baking sheet and bake in the preheated oven for 5 minutes, until browned and crispy.

To finish, spread a generous portion of the béchamel sauce on each piece of toast, then a sprinkle of the mixed topping cheeses. Bake in the preheated oven until golden brown on top; 5–7 minutes should do it.

Crab on toast

Crab is an incredibly versatile meat and delicious whether served cold in a sandwich, or hot on toast. White crabmeat can be very delicate in flavour, so I always use both white and brown crabmeat, which gives a good balance of flavour and texture.

PREPARE 10–15 MINUTES / COOK 8–9 MINUTES

1 loaf of ciabatta bread,
    thinly sliced into 12 slices
vegetable oil, for drizzling
table salt, for sprinkling
150 g/5 oz. white crabmeat
100 g/3½ oz. brown crabmeat
50 ml/3½ tablespoons double/
    heavy cream
smoked chipotle Tabasco sauce
50 g/generous ½ cup grated/
    shredded mild Cheddar cheese
50 g/⅔ cup finely grated
    Parmesan cheese

MAKES 12 TOASTS

Preheat the oven to 180°C (350°F) Gas 4.

On a non-stick baking sheet, arrange the slices of ciabatta bread. Drizzle the bread with a little vegetable oil and sprinkle with a few pinches of salt. Bake in the preheated oven for 5 minutes, until just crispy.

Remove the baking sheet from the oven and allow the toast to cool. Leave the oven on.

In a mixing bowl, mix the white and brown crabmeat thoroughly with a fork. Add the cream, a good splash of smoked chipotle Tabasco sauce and a pinch of salt. Mix together.

When you are ready to serve, put a heaped teaspoon of the crab mixture onto each slice of toast and spread it evenly. Sprinkle a little of each cheese on top and then bake in the preheated oven for 3–4 minutes, until the cheese has melted and the toast is golden.

Serve immediately.

Chicken liver pâté

Pâté is one of those dishes that you'll never buy again once you realize just how easy it is to make. This recipe makes a classic, smooth pâté, flavoured with brandy. You might like to try a coarser 'farmhouse pâté' or try adding other flavours and ingredients.

PREPARE 20 MINUTES / COOK 20 MINUTES

vegetable oil, for cooking
750 g/1 lb. 10 oz. chicken livers
50 ml/3½ tablespoons brandy
150 g/10 tablespoons butter
50 g/3½ tablespoons butter
250 ml/1 cup double/heavy cream
Tabasco sauce
Worcestershire sauce
1 teaspoon English mustard
1 teaspoon table salt, or to taste

TO SERVE
sliced bread, to toast

blowtorch
450-g/1-lb loaf pan or individual ramekin dishes, lined with clingfilm/ plastic wrap, leaving enough overlap to also cover the top

SERVES 12

Heat a large, heavy-bottomed frying pan/skillet over a medium heat, until a drop of water sizzles when dropped in it.

Add just enough oil to cover the base of the frying pan/ skillet, before adding the chicken livers. Fry them for a few minutes, until they are starting to brown in places but are not cooked through.

Add the brandy and light the alcohol fumes with a blowtorch (or the stovetop, if you have gas). Once the alcohol has burnt off, add 100 g/7 tablespoons butter. As the butter melts, scrape the bottom of the pan with a wooden spoon to loosen any cooking residue.

Place the cooked livers and all of the juices in a food processor and blitz to a purée. Add the cream and continue to blitz the mixture until it is smooth. Add the seasoning – a couple of good glugs of Tabasco and Worcestershire sauces, the mustard and salt, then taste and adjust to your preference.

Strain the paté to remove any small lumps by pushing it through a fine sieve/strainer using a flexible spatula. Spoon the paté into the lined loaf pan or ramekin dishes and press it into all of the corners. Level the top, melt the remaining butter and pour over the top. Seal by folding the clingfilm/plastic wrap over the top. Leave to cool for 20 minutes. Refrigerate for at least 4 hours.

Serve with slices of fresh toast.

Gentleman's relish tarts

Hot, salty, savoury and cheesy, these tarts are a treat for the more discerning amongst us.

PREPARE 30 MINUTES / COOK 17 MINUTES

16 thin slices of soft Milk Bread
  (see page 118)
whipped butter, for spreading
80 g/3 oz. Gentleman's Relish
  (see below)
2 eggs
a few drops of Tabasco sauce
50 g/²⁄₃ cup finely grated/shredded
  Parmesan cheese
50 g/generous ½ cup finely grated
  Cheddar cheese

GENTLEMAN'S RELISH
½ teaspoon ground mace
½ teaspoon ground cinnamon
½ teaspoon ground ginger
½ teaspoon ground white pepper
dash of vegetable oil
100 g/7 tablespoons butter,
  softened
100 g/3½ oz. drained anchovies,
  finely chopped
2 teaspoons small capers, drained
  and finely chopped
grated zest of 1 lemon

MAKES 1 JAR

sterilized 250-ml/1-cup resealable jar
2 non-stick 8-hole muffin trays

MAKES 8 TARTS

pictured page 134

For the Gentleman's Relish, heat a dry non-stick frying pan/skillet over a medium heat until it sizzles when a drop of water is placed in it. Place the mace, cinnamon, ginger and pepper in the hot frying pan/skillet and stir with a wooden spoon, then take off the heat immediately. Now add a dash of vegetable oil and cook the spices using the residual heat in the pan. Add the butter while the pan is still warm and stir until it is just melted. Add a little heat to the pan if necessary to melt the butter, but not enough to make it foam or cook.

Now add the chopped anchovies, capers and lemon zest and stir to combine. Pour the mixture into the sterilized jar. Place the jar in the refrigerator to cool and set the relish. Store in the refrigerator and use within 6 weeks.

Preheat the oven to 200°C (400°F) Gas 6.

To make the tart cases, trim the crusts off all of the bread slices. Butter the bread lightly on both sides and then place two slices in each of the muffin tray holes, set at 45° angles to each other. Once all of the holes are filled, place the other muffin tray directly on top and press down. This will force the bread into the muffin holes, forming cup shapes.

Place the two muffin trays, still pressed together, into the preheated oven. Place something heavy (a saucepan, for example) on top, to keep the trays under pressure.

Bake for 12 minutes, then remove the trays from the oven. Leave the oven on. Allow them to cool before removing the top muffin tray. Check the tart cases are formed and cooked.

To finish the tarts, place a generous dollop of the gentleman's relish into each tart case. Quickly whisk the eggs, then place 2 teaspoons of the whisked eggs into each case. Add a splash of Tabasco sauce and a generous sprinkle of the two grated/shredded cheeses.

Bake in the preheated oven for 5 minutes, before removing and checking that the egg has cooked. Serve hot or cold.

Cheese choux

This is a cheese-lover's dream. Mouthfuls of warm, mozzarella-filled,
cheesy pastry... amazing!

PREPARE 40 MINUTES / COOK 20 MINUTES

CHOUX PASTRY
75 g/½ cup strong bread flour
150 ml/⅔ cup water
75 g/5 tablespoons butter
2 eggs
50 g/⅔ cup finely grated/shredded
    Parmesan cheese

CHEESY CREAM
200 ml/generous ¾ cup double/
    heavy cream
100 g/3½ oz. mozzarella cheese
50 g/generous ½ cup finely grated/
    shredded Cheddar cheese

TOPPING
50 g/⅔ cup finely grated/shredded
    Parmesan cheese

*2 baking sheets lined with
    baking parchment*
disposable piping/pastry bag

MAKES 24

pictured page 135

Preheat the oven to 200°C (400°F) Gas 6.

For the choux pastry, place the flour in a stand mixer fitted with a pastry attachment and start mixing slowly.

In a large saucepan, heat the water and butter and bring to the boil. Take off the boil and immediately pour the hot mixture over the flour in the mixer. Beat the hot mixture using a medium speed, until it is all combined. Then, one at a time, add the eggs, while continuing to beat, until the pastry is smooth. Add the finely grated/shredded Parmesan and beat until combined.

Using a teaspoon, form balls of the choux pastry and place on the lined baking sheets, leaving a clear 2.5-cm/1-inch gap between them.

Bake in the preheated oven for about 15 minutes, until golden.

Remove from the oven and place on a wire rack to cool. Prick each choux bun with a small knife before placing on the rack (the hole will allow steam to escape and stop them becoming soggy).

For the cheesy cream, put the cream in a small saucepan and add the mozzarella (broken up into small pieces) and the Cheddar cheese. Warm the pan over a low heat, stirring continuously to form a thick, gooey, cheese sauce. Allow to cool for 10 minutes before putting the sauce into the piping/pastry bag.

Snip off the tip of the piping/pastry bag and squirt some cheesy cream into the centre of each choux bun through the hole you made to allow the steam to escape. The choux buns can be stored at this stage for a couple of days in the refrigerator.

To serve, sprinkle the choux buns with the grated/shredded Parmesan and bake in the preheated oven for 5 minutes. Serve hot.

Preserves & cordials

Bramble & rose jam/jelly

This was the first jam/jelly we made at the cafe. I wanted a traditional flavour with a hint of something memorable that would keep customers coming back for more. After much experimentation and testing, my jams/jellies are all made by weight, not temperature, so a decent pair of scales is important. We cook the mixture until about thirty percent of the total weight has boiled off; I find this leaves a much brighter flavour than boiling at a higher temperature. I have reduced the sugar content by about thirty percent in my recipes and make use of lemon instead of adding pectin, so the results are a little less firm than commercial jams/jellies, but the fruit has a fresher taste.

PREPARE 5 MINUTES / COOK 20–35 MINUTES

200 g/1½ cups blackberries
150 g/1½ cups strawberries
150 g/1½ cups redcurrants
350 g/1¾ cups caster/granulated sugar
70 g/scant ⅓ cup freshly squeezed lemon juice
1 teaspoon rose water

MAKES 650 G/500 ML/2 CUPS
JAM/JELLY

Place all the ingredients except the rose water into a large, heavy-bottomed saucepan and weigh the total weight (including the pan). From the total weight, subtract 300 g/ 10½ oz.; this will be your finished weight.

Bring the ingredients to a low simmer and continue to simmer until your finished weight is reached. This should take 20–35 minutes, depending on how high you simmer it. Stir the mixture regularly while it is simmering to stop it catching on the bottom of the pan.

Once the finished weight is reached, remove from the heat and add the rose water, then stir gently to combine thoroughly. This will make 2–3 jars of jam/jelly (500 ml/2 cups in total).

Clean, then sterilize the jars and lids by placing them in a preheated oven at 120°C (250°F) Gas ½ for at least 15 minutes. Carefully remove and then pour the jam/jelly in while everything is hot. Seal and leave to cool and set.

Once the jam/jelly has been opened, store in the refrigerator and use within 2 weeks.

Strawberry & elderflower jam/jelly

Strawberries and elderflower are the essence of an English Summer.
Wimbledon, cream teas, dappled sunlight and cricket on the green.
In this recipe, I have reduced the sugar to make the strawberry flavour
shine through, so the jam/jelly has a soft texture as a result.

PREPARE 5 MINUTES / COOK 20–35 MINUTES

500 g/2½ cups strawberries
350 g/1¾ cups caster/granulated
   sugar
70 g/scant ⅓ cup freshly squeezed
   lemon juice
100 ml/⅓ cup Elderflower Cordial
   (see page 148)

MAKES 670 G/520 ML/GENEROUS
2 CUPS JAM/JELLY

Place all the ingredients into a large, heavy-bottomed saucepan
and weigh the total weight, including the pan. From the total
weight, subtract 350 g/12 oz.; this will be your finished weight.

Bring the ingredients to a low simmer and continue to
simmer until your finished weight is reached (it will take
between 20–35 minutes depending how high you simmer it).
Stir the mixture regularly while it is simmering to stop it
catching on the bottom of the pan.

Once the finished weight is reached, remove from the heat
and allow to cool for 5 minutes. This will make 2–3 jars of jam/
jelly (520 ml/generous 2 cups in total).

Clean, then sterilize the jars and lids by placing them in a
preheated oven at 120°C (250°F) Gas ½ for at least 15 minutes.
Carefully remove then and pour the jam/jelly in while everything
is hot. Seal and leave to cool and set.

Once the jam/jelly has been opened, store in the refrigerator
and use within 2 weeks.

Orange & whiskey marmalade

This is not a recipe to be rushed. Slowly simmering the fruit means the peel is soft and not too bitter. Only half is used in the final marmalade; save the rest, as you can use it to make candied peel for cake decorations. This marmalade makes a great present for family and friends. Use 500-ml/2-cup clip top jars for a generous gift.

PREPARE 15 MINUTES / COOK 145 MINUTES

4 large oranges
   (preferably Seville oranges)
2.4 kg/12 cups sugar
grated zest and freshly squeezed
   juice of 2 lemons
100 ml/⅓ cup whiskey

MAKES ABOUT 1.5 KG/3½ LB.

Clean the oranges by pouring boiling water over them to remove any waxy coating. Cut the oranges into quarters then place them in a large pan and cover with 2 litres/quarts of water. Bring the water to a low simmer and leave at a low simmer for 1½ hours (keep the level of water topped up).

Pick out the orange segments and scoop out the pulp. Put the peel aside and return the pulp to the simmering liquid. Continue to simmer for a further 30 minutes. Strain the liquid to remove the pulp, then return the liquid to the pan. You should have about 2.5 litres/quarts in total. Slowly add the sugar, gently stirring to dissolve it all.

Thinly slice about half of the orange peel and add to the marmalade liquid. Add the lemon zest and juice and stir to combine.

Place a few clean teaspoons in your freezer. You'll need these to test whether the marmalade is set.

Bring the liquid back to a simmer and continue to simmer for 25 minutes. The marmalade is ready when the surface no longer froths when simmering, instead, it bubbles in a slow, almost relaxed way. With practice, you will know when the setting point is reached, but we will test it for now.

Test the marmalade is ready by dripping a little onto a frozen teaspoon. If it's ready, it will set in about 20 seconds; if it doesn't, simmer for a further 5 minutes and test again. Continue until it sets in 20 seconds.

Once the marmalade is ready, add the whiskey and stir through. Simmer for a couple of minutes to boil off the alcohol.

This makes just under 1.5 kg/3½ lb. of marmalade in total, so measure your jars for volume to ensure you have enough.

Clean, then sterilize the jars and lids by placing in a preheated oven at 120°C (250°F) Gas ½ for at least 15 minutes. Remove carefully and pour in the marmalade while everything is hot. Seal and leave to cool and set. Once the marmalade is opened, store in the refrigerator and use within 2 weeks.

Victoria plum jelly

There is an old railway line near me where I go to collect Victoria plums in the Autumn/Fall. They grow from plum stones/pits thrown out of the train windows in Victorian times, when it was usual to take a bowl of fruit on a day trip on the train. This recipe works with any plums, so buy the small or misshapen ones, in season, that no one else wants – they make the best jams/jellies. If you don't have a juicer, cook the plums on a low heat until they form a mash, then sieve/strain to extract the juice.

PREPARE 15 MINUTES / COOK 20–35 MINUTES

approx. 800 g/1¾ lb. plums
400 g/2 cups caster/granulated
　sugar
70 g/scant ⅓ cup freshly squeezed
　lemon juice

juicer

MAKES 520 ML/GENEROUS 2 CUPS

Stone/pit the plums by cutting right around each plum, top to bottom, then twist to separate the two halves and remove the stone/pit. Pass the stoned/pitted plums through the juicer to make 500 ml/2 cups of plum juice.

Into a large, heavy-bottomed saucepan, pour 500 ml/2 cups of the plum juice, then add the sugar and lemon juice.

Weigh the total weight, including the pan. From the total weight, subtract 300 g/10½ oz.; this will be your finished weight.

Bring the ingredients to a low simmer and continue to stir and simmer until your finished weight is reached (it will take 20–35 minutes depending on how high you simmer it). Stir the mixture regularly while it is simmering to stop it catching on the bottom of the pan.

Once the finished weight is reached, remove from the heat and allow to cool for 5 minutes.

Clean, then sterilize the jars and lids by placing them in a preheated oven at 120°C (250°F) Gas ½ for at least 15 minutes. Remove carefully and pour the jelly in while everything is hot. Seal and leave to cool and set.

Once the jelly has been opened, store in the refrigerator and use within 2 weeks.

Apple & lavender jelly

Lavender is one of my favourite aromatic ingredients and it's delicious with cheese, creating a nice alternative to chutney. I have used agar-agar to set the jelly, which makes a firm jelly that holds well on a warm plate and has the advantage of being vegetarian. Lavender extract can be bought from most good baking shops and websites.

PREPARE 5 MINUTES / COOK 5 MINUTES

500 ml/2 cups fresh apple juice
7 g/¼ oz. agar-agar powder
culinary lavender extract, to taste

MAKES 500 ML/2 CUPS

Place the apple juice into a saucepan and bring to a low simmer. Sprinkle the agar-agar powder on top of the simmering juice and leave it to dissolve. Gently whisk, if needed, to combine it fully. Simmer for a further 5 minutes.

Take off the heat and add some lavender extract, then taste. I add about 10 drops, but culinary extracts come in varying strengths, so don't be surprised if you need to add double that. The lavender should taste like a background flavour against the fresh apple.

Clean, then sterilize the jars and lids by placing them in a preheated oven at 120°C (250°F) Gas ½ for at least 15 minutes. Remove carefully and pour the jelly in while everything is hot. Seal and leave to cool and set.

Once the jelly has been opened, store in a refrigerator and use within 2 weeks.

pictured page 145

Lemon & mandarin curd

This recipe is a variation of a traditional lemon curd, where I have replaced one lemon with two mandarins to make a softer flavour, more suited to afternoon tea.

PREPARE 15 MINUTES / COOK 10 MINUTES

grated zest and freshly squeezed
   juice of 2 mandarin oranges
grated zest of 1 lemon
freshly squeezed juice of 3 lemons
100 g/7 tablespoons butter
250 g/1¼ cups caster/granulated
   sugar
3 eggs
1 egg yolk

MAKES 500 ML/2 CUPS

Place all the ingredients in a non-stick saucepan and mix using a hand blender. Place the saucepan on a medium heat whilst continuing to mix with the hand blender. When the ingredients reach just over 80°C/176°F they will thicken into a curd. Take off the heat, but continue to use the hand blender for a couple of minutes while it cools a little.

Clean, then sterilize two jars and lids by placing them in a preheated oven at 120°C (250°F) Gas ½ for at least 15 minutes. Remove carefully and pour the curd in while everything is hot. Seal and leave to cool and set. Once the curd has been opened, store in the refrigerator and use within 2 weeks.

Plum curd

Choose purple plums, as they will make a stunning purple curd. Choose plums that are just ripe to get the sharp sourness that a good curd needs.

PREPARE 5 MINUTES / COOK 10 MINUTES

500 g/1 lb. 2 oz. plums
freshly squeezed juice of 1 lemon
100 g/7 tablespoons butter
250 g/1¼ cups caster/granulated
   sugar
3 eggs
1 egg yolk

juicer

MAKES 500 ML/2 CUPS

Stone/pit the plums. Pass the stoned/pitted plums through the juicer to make 300 ml/1¼ cups of plum juice.

Place all the ingredients in a non-stick saucepan and mix using a hand blender. Place the saucepan on a medium heat whilst continuing to mix with the hand blender.

When the ingredients reach just over 80°C/176°F they will thicken into a curd. Take off the heat, but continue to use the hand blender for a couple of minutes while it cools a little.

Clean, then sterilize two jars and lids by placing them in a preheated oven at 120°C (250°F) Gas ½ for at least 15 minutes. Remove carefully and pour the curd in while everything is hot. Seal and leave to cool and set. Once the curd has been opened, store in the refrigerator and use within 2 weeks.

Blueberry cordial

Blueberries have a lovely sweet flavour, so this is a great recipe for children who have a sweet tooth. I love this cordial in cocktails; it mixes very well with rum or vodka.

PREPARE 10 MINUTES / COOK 45 MINUTES

750 g/6 cups blueberries
250 g/1¼ cups caster/granulated sugar
grated zest and freshly squeezed juice of 2 lemons

MAKES ABOUT 1 LITRE/QUART

pictured page 150

In a saucepan, place all of the ingredients, along with 500 ml/2 cups of water. Bring to a low simmer for 30 minutes, then mash the ingredients to extract the flavour.

Line a sieve/strainer with fine muslin/cheesecloth or a spotlessly clean cotton cloth. Pour the mixture through the lined sieve/strainer into another saucepan (don't press or squash the ingredients, or the cordial will be cloudy). If it needs longer, leave it to drip through the sieve/strainer overnight in the refrigerator.

When it has finished draining, bring the liquid to a simmer, then decant into a pasteurized bottle, seal and cool.

Once opened, store in the refrigerator and use within 2 weeks.

Elderflower cordial

I love elderflower as a flavour and use it in baking and desserts, as well as cocktails.

PREPARE 20 MINUTES / COOK 20 MINUTES

approx. 20 elderflower heads
grated zest and freshly squeezed juice of 4 lemons, plus extra juice to taste
4 litres/quarts just-boiled water
1 kg/5 cups caster/granulated sugar

MAKES ABOUT 4 LITRES/QUARTS

pictured page 150

In a bucket-sized container, place the elderflower heads, lemon zest and juice. Pour the just-boiled water into the container, covering them. Use a saucepan lid to hold the flower heads under the water. Leave to infuse for at least 2 hours.

Line a sieve/strainer with fine muslin/cheesecloth or a spotlessly clean cotton cloth. Pour the mixture through the lined sieve/strainer into another saucepan. Do this in batches if you don't have a big enough pan.

When it has finished draining, bring the liquid to a simmer and add the sugar, dissolving it all to make the cordial.

Check the flavour and add a little extra lemon juice, if needed, before decanting into pasteurized bottles. Seal and cool.

Once opened, store in the refrigerator and use within 2 weeks.

Rhubarb & ginger cordial

This cordial, mixed with gin and tonic, is the perfect accompaniment to afternoon tea.

PREPARE 10 MINUTES / COOK 45 MINUTES

600 g/1 lb. 5 oz. rhubarb stalks,
   roughly chopped
400 g/2 cups caster/granulated
   sugar
grated zest and freshly squeezed
   juice of 2 lemons
100 g/3½ oz. fresh root ginger,
   grated

MAKES ABOUT 1 LITRE/QUART

pictured page 150

Place all of the ingredients in a saucepan along with 600 ml/2½ cups of water. Bring to a low simmer for 30 minutes, then mash the ingredients to extract the flavour.

Line a sieve/strainer with fine muslin/cheesecloth or a spotlessly clean cotton cloth. Pour the mixture through the lined sieve/strainer into another saucepan (don't press or squash the ingredients, or the cordial will be cloudy). If it needs longer, leave it to drip through the sieve/strainer overnight in the refrigerator. When it has finished draining, bring the liquid to a simmer, then decant into a pasteurized bottle, then seal and cool. Once opened, store in the refrigerator and use within 2 weeks.

Apple & pear cordial

The smell of apples and pears, with a hint of cinnamon, always makes me think of Christmas. Using green apples keeps this cordial bright and fresh.

PREPARE 10 MINUTES / COOK 30 MINUTES

500 g/1 lb. 2 oz. green apples,
   roughly chopped
500 g/1 lb. 2 oz. pears, roughly
   chopped
250 g/1¼ cups brown sugar
grated zest and freshly squeezed
   juice of 1 lemon
a pinch of ground cinnamon

MAKES ABOUT 1 LITRE/QUART

pictured page 150

In a saucepan, place all of the ingredients, along with 600 ml/2½ cups of water. Bring to a low simmer for 30 minutes, then mash the ingredients to extract the flavour.

Line a sieve/strainer with fine muslin/cheesecloth or a spotlessly clean cotton cloth. Pour the mixture through the lined sieve/strainer into another saucepan (don't press or squash the ingredients, or the cordial will be cloudy). If it needs longer, leave it to drip through the sieve/strainer overnight in the refrigerator.

When it has finished draining, bring the liquid to a simmer, then decant into a pasteurized bottle, seal and cool.

Once opened, store in the refrigerator and use within 2 weeks.

Raspberry & blackcurrant cordial

Bursting with goodness and flavour, the mix of raspberries and blackcurrants in this recipe is a combination that works brilliantly.

PREPARE 10 MINUTES / COOK 45 MINUTES

400 g/3 cups raspberries
350 g/3½ cups blackcurrants
350 g/1¾ cups sugar
grated zest and freshly squeezed
    juice of 2 lemons

MAKES ABOUT 1 LITRE/QUART

pictured page 151

Place all of the ingredients in a saucepan along with 500 ml/2 cups of water. Bring to a low simmer for 30 minutes, then mash the ingredients to extract the flavour.

Line a sieve/strainer with fine muslin/cheesecloth or a spotlessly clean cotton cloth. Pour the mixture through the lined sieve/strainer into another saucepan (don't press or squash the ingredients, or the cordial will be cloudy). If it needs longer, leave it to drip through the sieve/strainer overnight in the refrigerator.

When it has finished draining, bring the liquid to a simmer, then decant into a pasteurized bottle, seal and cool.

Once opened, store in the refrigerator and use within 2 weeks.

Homemade lemonade

Lemonade is not just lemon juice and water, a great lemonade involves using the whole lemon and has bitterness from the pith and intensity from the zest... you may never be able to buy lemonade again.

PREPARE 15 MINUTES

1 lemon
freshly squeezed juice of 2 lemons
    (100 ml/⅓ cup)
100 g/½ cup caster/granulated
    sugar
a pinch of table salt
850 ml/3½ cups ice cold water

MAKES ABOUT 1 LITRE/QUART

Place the lemon in a bowl, then pour boiling water over to cover it. Leave for 10 minutes to dissolve any wax and soften the lemon skin.

Remove the lemon from the hot water and place it in a food processor. Add the lemon juice, sugar, salt and about 200 ml/generous ¾ cup of the ice cold water. Blitz for 5 minutes to make a strong lemon juice.

If you prefer your lemonade without bits in it, strain it through a sieve/strainer.

Pour the juice into a jug/pitcher and top up with the remaining ice cold water. Stir and serve.

Gin

Like any civilized person, I love a good-quality gin. Even more, I enjoy making my own gin flavours and here are several recipes to try for yourself. I suggest buying a couple of bottles of decent gin, three 500-ml/2-cup clip-top jars and make all three of these recipes as a starting point. You then have the basis of a good ending to your afternoon tea as everyone relaxes and samples the different flavours!

PREPARE 10 MINUTES / INFUSE 2 WEEKS MINIMUM

RHUBARB GIN
150 g/5 oz. fresh rhubarb
100 g/½ cup caster/granulated
   sugar
1 litre/quart gin
fresh mint, to serve
tonic water, to serve

CUCUMBER GIN
1 medium cucumber
table salt
1 litre/quart gin
fresh borage flowers and cucumber
   slices, to serve
tonic water, to serve

BRAMBLE GIN
200 g/7 oz. mixed berries
1 litre/1 quart gin
100 g/½ cup caster/granulated
   sugar
1 teaspoon rose water
lemon slices, to serve
tonic water, to serve

3 x 500-ml/2-cup clip-top jars

Clean, then sterilize the jars, and lids by placing in a preheated oven at 120°C (250°F) Gas ½ for at least 15 minutes before you add the ingredients.

Rhubarb gin
Slice the rhubarb into even pieces about 1 cm/½ inch long, and place in a sterilized jar. Add the sugar, then fill with gin. Seal and leave to infuse for at least a couple of weeks. Agitate the jar gently every few days.

After a couple of weeks, sample and add a little more sugar if needed. Serve with a sprig of fresh mint.

Cucumber gin
Clean the cucumber, then peel in even slices. Place the slices in a sterilized jar with a couple of large pinches of table salt, then fill with gin. Seal and leave to infuse for at least a couple of weeks. Agitate the jar gently every few days.

After a couple of weeks, sample and add a little more salt if needed. Serve with fresh borage flowers and a slice of cucumber.

Bramble gin
Place the berries in a sterilized jar. Add the sugar to the jar, then fill with gin. Seal and leave to infuse for at least a couple of weeks. Agitate the jar gently every few days.

After a couple of weeks, add the rose water and agitate to combine fully. Taste and add a little more sugar if needed.

Serve with a slice of lemon.

Serve each gin with a little ice; 30 ml/1 fl. oz./2 tablespoons of gin to 150 ml/5 fl. oz./⅔ cup of good-quality tonic water.

Mat's fizz

This is the drink we toast in the New Year with. This quick and easy cocktail balances the slight bitterness of prosecco with the sweet and floral flavours of lavender and elderflower. It's the perfect celebration of English flowers.

PREPARE 2 MINUTES

**20 ml/4 teaspoons Elderflower
   Cordial (see page 148)**
**2 teaspoons lavender cordial
   or a few drops of lavender extract**
100 ml/¹/₃ cup prosecco

SERVES 1

Into your champagne glass, pour the elderflower and lavender cordials, then add the prosecco.

Stir with a cocktail stirrer to combine.

Serve immediately.

Rhubarb fizz

Rhubarb fizz has a stunning pink colour yet tastes both sweet and a little spicy from the ginger; it contrasts well with the pale blue of the Mat's Fizz for functions and events.

PREPARE 2 MINUTES

**30 ml/1 fl. oz. Rhubarb & Ginger
   Cordial (see page 149)**
100 ml/¹/₃ cup prosecco
a strip of lemon peel

SERVES 1

Into your champagne glass, pour the cordial, then add the prosecco.

Stir with a cocktail stick to combine.

Wipe the rim of the glass with the lemon peel, then twist it over the drink to release the aroma before placing into the cocktail.

Serve immediately.

Index

Acknowledgements

I couldn't write this book without the ongoing tasting, testing and editing assistance of my wife Amanda, she has given up a large part of her annual holidays to see this book finished and makes me look like a far better writer and cook than I really am, thank you Amanda.

The photography and styling by Steve Painter is some of his best in my opinion and the styling by Lucy McElvie and Katy Gilhooly makes the food look amazing. My editors, Miriam, Kate and Julia are too patient and an absolute pleasure to work with, thank you for the opportunity to write another book with you.